THE ILLUSTRATED

Bible-Based

DICTIONARY

of

DREAM SYMBOLS

THE ILLUSTRATED

Bible-Based

DICTIONARY

of

DREAM SYMBOLS

Dr. Joe Ibojie

Illustrations by Mark Szarlos-Farkas'.

DESTINY IMAGE EUROPE™ srl
Via Maiella, 1
66020 San Giovanni Teatino (Ch) - Italy

"Changing the world, one book at a time."

ISBN 10: 88-89127-14-7
ISBN 13: 978-88-89127-14-8

For Worldwide Distribution, Printed in Italy.

2 3 4 5 6 7 8 / 10 09 08 07

This book and all other Destiny Image Europe™ books are available at Christian bookstores and distributors worldwide.

To order products, or for any other correspondence:

DESTINY IMAGE EUROPE™ srl
Via Acquacorrente, 6
65123 - Pescara - Italy
Tel. +39 085 4716623 - Fax: +39 085 4716622
E-mail: info@eurodestinyimage.com

Or reach us on the Internet:

www.eurodestinyimage.com

ENDORSEMENTS

This is a wonderful resource to assist the reader in understanding the symbolic language of dreams. Dr. Ibojie uses the Scripture extensively to reveal spiritual truth and has compiled an extremely thorough resource for interpreting the significance of the different aspects of our dreams. God's gift on his life for understanding dreams is evident as he gives insight to the subject. This is a must-add to your personal library as an active member of the Body of Christ.

Emmanuel Ziga, President
Grace For All Nations Ministries International
Seattle, Washington

The Illustrated Bible-Based Dictionary of Dream Symbols and *Dreams and Visions: How to Receive, Interpret and Apply Your Dreams* are mighty tools in the hands of those in the Body of Christ who are seeking to recognize the voice of God in their lives. God has blessed Dr. Ibojie not only with a powerful anointing and gift himself, but also with the grace to help others unlock the inner potential within themselves through powerful keys of wisdom and insight. These books are treasure chests, loaded down with revelation and the hidden mysteries of God that have been waiting since before the foundation of the earth to be uncovered. *The Illustrated Bible-Based Dictionary of Dream Symbols* shall bless, strengthen, and guide any believer who is in search for the purpose, promise, and destiny of God for their lives. Thank God for this Christ-centred, Bible-based message that will restore the awareness that God is continually longing to communicate His love, desires, and will to His children. *"He that keeps Israel never sleeps or slumbers."* While you are sleeping, He is still speaking. Let he who has an ear (the desire to hear) hear what the Spirit is saying to the Church.

Bishop Ron Scott, Jr.
President, Kingdom Coalition International
Hagerstown, Maryland

The Illustrated Bible-Based Dictionary of Dream Symbols is much more than just a handbook for dream symbols; it has also added richness to our reading of God's Word. This book has many great God-inspired strategies to understand the symbols in the ever-increasing dreams and visions the Lord is using to speak to His people. Whether you use this book to assist in interpreting your dreams or as a companion for your study of the Word of God, you will find Dr. Joe's book to be a welcome companion.

Robert & Joyce Ricciardelli
Directors, Visionary Advancement Strategies
Seattle, Washington

On our flight from Amsterdam to Florida, I sat beside Joe Ibojie. Joe obviously thought he would opt for the reading method of passing time, as he had a few books tucked under his arm. One of these books was his draft of a dictionary of dream symbolism. He was going through it, cross-referencing each definition with the Bible and adding annotations where necessary. In no time at all the conversation turned to dreams and all books were put to the side. The next eight hours passed so quickly that we could hardly believe it when we landed in Miami. In fact, throughout the following two weeks, as Joe and I shared a room and ministered together, the conversation would always turn to dreams and visions. Little did I know that the content of most of our friendly chats since then would make it to the pages of his wonderful book. Not that my contribution was anything more than asking Joe difficult questions, but I was pleased to see that his answers to these questions are contained in this book.

I have been privileged to minister with Joe on a frequent basis, but I am more privileged to know him not just as a person with Daniel-type anointing or as a prophetic voice (although he is frequently both these things to me), but as one of my closest friends. He is a true servant of

God and a man with a passion to see God's Kingdom extend to wherever he goes and whomever he meets. Writing this book is simply an extension of this passion and has come out of years of experience—of working it out on a practical level, of seeing people transformed and set free to a life of liberty and purpose in the Holy Spirit, and of seeing people built up, encouraged, and edified, because they have come to a clearer understanding of God's purposes and plans in their life through a godly and, I believe, biblical interpretation of their dreams.

Pastor Phil Sanderson
All Nations Christian Fellowship
Aberdeen, Scotland, United Kingdom

I've had some amazing dreams recently that have been great confirmations for me, and *The Illustrated Bible-Based Dictionary of Dream Symbols* is fantastic in helping me make sense of them all—it's been a real blessing to me.

Jess Howell, Editor
Maidstone, Kent, United Kingdom

CONTENTS

FOREWORDS

…Write down the revelation and make it plain on tablets so that a herald may run with it. For the revelation awaits an appointed time; it speaks of the end and will not prove false. Though it linger, wait for it; it will certainly come and will not delay (Habakkuk 2:2-3).

The first time I met Dr. Joe Ibojie was in Aberdeen city on an extremely cold evening when the sky was dark with impending snow. By contrast, Joe's countenance was bright and sunny and in all of our ensuing dialogue, whether in person, by telephone or email, I have found Joe's love for Christ and for life to be a constant source of joy.

Joe and his wife, Cynthia, and their four delightful children warmly welcomed me into their hearts and their home. It was at their family home that I had my first taste of African food—delicious! As a medical practitioner, Joe's life is full and busy. Not only this, but he and Cynthia have recently become pastors of The Father's House, a Christian fellowship in Aberdeen. I believe in "meeting the man behind the ministry," and I am delighted to commend Dr. Joe Ibojie to you as a loving husband, father, doctor, teacher, brother, and friend as well as a gifted Christian writer. He is a genuine and humble Christian leader. I am sure you will be blessed by his character and desire to serve the Lord.

I have enjoyed ministering with Joe. He is enthusiastic and energetic and is an anointed teacher on the subject of dreams and their interpretation. Joe's inspiration is ever our Lord Jesus Christ.

About the Book

Over the last year it has been a wonderful experience to journey with Joe as he has worked on his first two books, *The Illustrated Bible-Based Dictionary of Dream Symbols* being the companion to *Dreams and Visions: How to Receive, Interpret and Apply Your Dreams.* I have thoroughly enjoyed learning more about dreams and their interpretation as we have fellowshipped, studied the Scriptures, and prayed together. Joe's teaching is motivational.

The Illustrated Bible-Based Dictionary of Dream Symbols is written in clear language, with detailed descriptions throughout its narrative that assist the reader on the journey of discovering the gift of interpretation. Dr. Joe enables the reader to become conversant with the parabolic language of symbols through Holy Spirit-inspired articulation. We rejoice that our Lord in His infinite grace and mercy chooses to communicate with His children. Ultimately, the gift of God's revelation ought to draw us deeper into a loving relationship with Christ, His Church, and those who do not yet know Him

The Illustrated Bible-Based Dictionary of Dream Symbols is not intended to be a stand-alone resource; in other words, interpretation of symbols is not to be seen as a prescriptive exercise. Without prayerful application and understanding, our attempts at interpretation would be little more than presumptive. We may rest in the reality that interpretations belong to God (see Gen. 40:8). Joe encourages the reader to approach dream interpretation from a worshipful posture, giving careful consideration to the context and content of each dream or revelatory experience (such as a vision). Interpretation cannot be seen as a formula, but rather we ought to receive it as a gift from God, whereby the Holy Spirit imparts wisdom and understanding, fusing them with our faith, and opens our surrendered hearts and minds to receive Divine Counsel in a way that we can readily apply the interpretation of the dream symbols to our modern lifestyles.

The Illustrated Bible-Based Dictionary of Dream Symbols is a useful resource to help train and equip the Church to demonstrate God's love to the many who have not yet received salvation.

Jesus spoke in the language of parables and symbols to His disciples and to the multitudes who followed Him. Our Lord used numerous images to describe what the Kingdom of Heaven is like, such as a field (see Mt. 13:24), a mustard seed (see Mt. 13:31), treasure hidden in a field (Mt 13:44), and a net let down into the lake that catches all kinds of fish (see Mt. 13:47). Jesus asked His disciples, *"Have you understood all these things?" They replied "yes." Jesus then responded, "Therefore every teacher of the law who has been instructed about the kingdom of heaven is like the owner of a house who brings out of his storeroom new treasures as well as old"* (Mt. 13:52).

My prayer for you, dear reader, is that you will gain understanding by the Holy Spirit from *The Illustrated Bible-Based Dictionary of Dream Symbols* and that you will enjoy this new treasure that the Lord has poured out from Heaven's storeroom through his servant, Dr. Joe Ibojie.

We live to glorify our heavenly Father. Don't be disappointed if it takes a little time and effort to grow in your gifting. Jesus is patient and gracious as He trains us in His ways. Be blessed!

Catherine Brown, servant of Christ
Author of *The Normal, the Deep and the Crazy* and
Confessions of a Fasting Housewife

Gatekeepers Prayer & Mission
Million Hours of Praise
Glasgow, UK

God has given Joe wisdom to open a door for us to understand the symbolic nature of our dreams. Both Joe and I have been students of John Paul Jackson Schools of Dreams and Visions. John Paul says 98 percent of our dreams are on personal issues and dreams are not to be taken literally, but are symbolic and must be interpreted.

This book is a companion to *Dreams and Visions: How to Receive, Interpret and Apply Your Dreams* and will help you gain depth and breadth of understanding in what these symbols mean. When Joe teaches, he often asks questions like, "What do you think it means?" and what it means to you may be different from what it means for someone else.

We have a tool in our hands that can help take away the frustration of not knowing what our dreams mean and also remove the danger of misinterpretation. I thank God and the Holy Spirit for my friend Joe Ibojie and for the many gifts and talents he has.

Out of Joe's anointing God has led him to write these books in order that we may grow in our understanding. I pray as you read that God will bless you and give you wisdom as you use these wonderful tools.

Pastor Joseph Ewen
Founder and Leader of Riverside Church Network
Banff, Scotland, United Kingdom

PART 1

SYMBOLS

CHAPTER 1

Introduction to Symbols

A symbol is an image that stands for something in addition to its literal meaning. It therefore has more meaning than just its simple literal meaning on its own in the natural run of things. In practical terms, symbols are things that represent or stand for something else, or are used to typify something else, either by association, resemblance, or convention. A symbol can also mean a material object used to represent something invisible, such as an idea (e.g., the dove as a symbol of peace).

How Symbols Derive Their Meaning

A message that is given in symbols automatically switches your thinking to symbolism. Every parable needs to be symbolically interpreted and the meaning should be drawn for each symbol. (A parable language is when symbols are used to represent things.) Symbols are not real entities; they are simply representations of the real entities. The meaning of a symbol is drawn first of all from the reservoir of the Word of God, then from the inherent meaning of the symbol or its association to the dreamer's experience, or from the culture and colloquial expressions in society.

In general terms, interpretation is the deciphering of a parable language that involves:

- Bringing meaning to the symbols in the dream and then gaining understanding of the message in the dream. Deriving the meanings for symbols should first of all be hinged on the Word of God;

this process also brings understanding to the symbolic actions in the dream.

• Expounding on the relevance of the symbols and the message of the dream to the dreamer's life circumstance. Exposition is bringing understanding to the symbols and events as they relate to the dreamer's personal experience. Exposition centers on the dreamer's experience.

• The deriving of the meaning for the symbols and the exposition must go together to truly interpret a dream or vision. Therefore, the true and complete interpretation must incorporate the two phases as well as be drawn in the following order:

   * The Scriptures.

   * The inherent meaning of the symbol.

   * The dreamer's personal experience.

   * The social influences of the dreamer (the culture and the colloquial expressions the dreamer is used to).

A symbol does not mean the same thing all the time and therefore the meaning of a symbol must be drawn for each dream. Remember, the true meaning of a symbol in a dream does not come from human reasoning or intellectualism, but by allowing the meaning to flow into our hearts or subconscious mind from the Holy Spirit. This inflow into our hearts occurs by being quiet and still in the inner being. The choice of symbols in the dream is very specific and purposeful, and it is the prerogative of God. A dream is therefore the truest representation of the situation because it is God's perspective of it; a dream addresses the issue more frankly than human illustration.

Why God Uses Symbols

• They help us to see the real thing from God's perspective because the symbol shows God's thinking.

• Striking features of symbols help the impartation and interpretation.

• The hidden meaning of the symbol allows God to clarify things in stages.

- Humility is the key, as it increases your dependence on the Holy Spirit. *"To keep me from becoming conceited **because of these surpassingly great revelations,** there was given me a thorn in my flesh, a messenger of satan, to torment me. Three times I pleaded with the Lord to take it away from me. But He said to me, 'My grace is sufficient for you, for My power is made perfect in weakness.' Therefore I will boast all the more gladly about my weaknesses, so that Christ's power may rest on me"* (2 Corinthians 12:7-9, emphasis added).

- The Lord will relate to a person in symbolism that has meaning to him/her. Dreams are a form of communication, an intimate language between the dreamer and the Lord.

- They secure the message from the enemies.

- They make you want to search out the meaning.

- The language of symbols is deep and powerful; at the same time it's the most elementary language of men and therefore available to all ages.

- The human mind understands or reads in pictures.

CHAPTER 2

UNDERSTANDING THE LANGUAGE OF SYMBOLS

(The Language of the Spirit)

The language of the spirit is the language of symbolism and no other book speaks in symbols more than the Bible. Symbolism is also the language of dreams and in several ways the language pattern in dreams is akin to the pattern of speech used in the Bible. Some people have described the Old Testament as the New Testament concealed because of the extensive use of symbolism.

The language of reason is limited whereas the language of symbols is infinite. Though a symbol may be identified by one word, it may also take volumes to be comprehensively described. There is great depth and power to the language of symbols and symbolic actions. As the saying goes, a picture is worth a thousand words. Children learn the language of pictures and symbols before they learn the language of words and reason. Man thinks and processes information in pictures.

God Himself described His pattern of speech to the prophets in Numbers:

He said, "Listen to My words: When a prophet of the Lord is among you, I reveal Myself to him in visions, I speak to him in dreams. But this is not true of My servant Moses; he is faithful in all My house. With him I speak face to face, clearly and not in riddles; he sees the form of the Lord. Why then were you not afraid to speak against My servant Moses?" (Numbers 12:6-8)

Key points from the above passage are:

• God does not speak to everyone the same way.

• He speaks in dreams and visions.

• He speaks in clear language.

• He speaks in riddles or parables.

• He speaks in dark speeches.

• He speaks in similitude.

He is God; therefore, He may choose how He speaks to us.

Jesus Christ revealed the secrets of the Kingdom of God only to the disciples and He also explained why He spoke and taught in parables:

> *The disciples came to Him and asked, "Why do You speak to the people in parables?" He replied, "The knowledge of the secrets of the kingdom of heaven has been given to you, but not to them. Whoever has will be given more, and he will have abundance. Whoever does not have, even what he has will be taken from him. This is why I speak to them in parables: 'Though seeing, they do not see; though hearing, they do not hear or understand'"* (Matthew 13:10-13).

Notice from the passage that parables were available to all people. Just as it was in those days the parable language of God (dreams) is available to everyone today, but the *heathen will "see and hear" without gaining understanding of the dreams.*

Jesus taught in parables and used symbols to illustrate His message:

> *With many similar parables Jesus spoke the word to them, as much as they could understand.* **He did not say anything to them without using a parable.** *But when He was alone with His own disciples, He explained everything* (Mark 4:33-34, emphasis added).

Jesus also described the role of the Holy Spirit in the understanding of what God says; that is, the Holy Spirit will explain the dark speeches, similitude, and parables of God to us (see Jn. 14:25-27).

Let us look at this passage and the wisdom keys inherent in them:

> *All this I have spoken while still with you. But the Counselor, the Holy Spirit, whom the Father will send in My name, will teach you all things and will remind you of everything I have said to you. Peace I leave with you; My peace I give you. I do not give to you as the world gives. Do not let your hearts be troubled and do not be afraid* (John 14:25-27).

From this passage it is clear to see that the Holy Spirit helps us by explaining parable language to us; without this, we will be unable to understand the mind of God on the issue.

CHAPTER 3

THE POWER OF THE LANGUAGE OF SYMBOLS

Those who have understood the tremendous power of symbols have gained incredible insight into the mysteries of God, because God's ways are wrapped up in the language of symbolism. Human beings think in pictures and people need visual appreciation in order to grasp the essence of a concept. Symbols evoke powerful emotion and elicit strong passion; from generation to generation, politicians, philosophers, and religious leaders have used them to illustrate their points. For example, national commitment is symbolized in the pride and honor that is accorded to the national symbol in the form of a flag. Many would be outraged to see their flag dishonored, and public hatred is often demonstrated by the burning of an enemy's national flag.

David—A Biblical Example

Symbolism brought the seriousness of David's adulterous act to him. Nathan's message to King David could have easily been a perfect setting for the plotting of a dream and God could have chosen to send King David the same message through a dream. Nathan narrated the message to David in a dream format, in parable, to bring home the gravity of the sin.

The Lord sent Nathan to David. When he came to him, he said, "There were two men in a certain town, one rich and the other poor. The rich man had a very large number of sheep and cattle, but the poor man had nothing except one little ewe lamb he had bought. He raised it, and it grew up with him and his children. It shared his food, drank from his cup and even

slept in his arms. It was like a daughter to him. Now a traveler came to
the rich man, but the rich man refrained from taking one of his own sheep
or cattle to prepare a meal for the traveler who had come to him. Instead,
he took the ewe lamb that belonged to the poor man and prepared it for
the one who had come to him." David burned with anger against the man
and said to Nathan, "As surely as the Lord lives, the man who did this
deserves to die! He must pay for that lamb four times over, because he did
such a thing and had no pity." Then Nathan said to David, "You are the
man! This is what the Lord, the God of Israel, says: 'I anointed you king
over Israel, and I delivered you from the hand of Saul. I gave your master's house to you, and your master's wives into your arms. I gave you the
house of Israel and Judah. And if all this had been too little, I would have
given you even more. Why did you despise the word of the Lord by doing
what is evil in His eyes? You struck down Uriah the Hittite with the sword
and took his wife to be your own. You killed him with the sword of the
Ammonites'" (2 Samuel 12:1-9).

Anatomy of Nathan's Statement to David

SYMBOL / ACTION	MEANING	THE POWER OF IMAGERY
Rich man.	David.	Important personality.
Poor man.	Uriah.	A person who is vulnerable because he lacks the necessities of life.
Little ewe, like a daughter.	Uriah's wife—precious to him.	Something precious to the dreamer.
Arrival of traveler.	A need arises.	A potential need is imminent or at hand.
Refrain from using his own.	Selfishness.	Spirit of self-centeredness, or inconsiderate of others.
David's anger burned against the injustice of the man in Nathan's story.	Then David came to a realization that the sin was his, therefore realizing the true gravity of the sin.	Holy anger stirred by spirit of righteousness or coming to one's senses after a period of attack of carnality.

CHAPTER 4

HOW TO DERIVE MEANING FROM PARABLE LANGUAGE

The Parable of the Sower

Then He told them many things in parables, saying: "A farmer went out to sow his seed. As he was scattering the seed, some fell along the path, and the birds came and ate it up. Some fell on rocky places, where it did not have much soil. It sprang up quickly, because the soil was shallow. But when the sun came up, the plants were scorched, and they withered because they had no root. Other seed fell among thorns, which grew up and choked the plants. Still other seed fell on good soil, where it produced a crop—a hundred, sixty or thirty times what was sown. He who has ears, let him hear" (Matthew 13:3-9).

The Interpretation

Listen then to what the parable of the sower means: When anyone hears the message about the kingdom and does not understand it, the evil one comes and snatches away what was sown in his heart. This is the seed sown along the path. The one who received the seed that fell on rocky places is the man who hears the word and at once receives it with joy. But since he has no root, he lasts only a short time. When trouble or persecution comes because of the word, he quickly falls away. The one who received the seed that fell among the thorns is the man who hears the word, but the worries of this life and the deceitfulness of wealth choke it, making it unfruitful. But the one who received the seed that fell on good soil is the man who hears the word and understands it. He produces a crop, yielding a hundred, sixty or thirty times what was sown (Matthew 13:18-23).

The Anatomy of the Parable of the Sower

SYMBOL	MEANING	DERIVED DREAM SYMBOL
Seed.	Word of God.	Word of God; God's promises, (something capable of multiplication).
Soil.	Heart of Man.	Potential for multiplication, either good or bad; the essence of life.
Farmer.	Jesus Christ.	God, pastor, spiritual leaders.
"Sown along the paths."	No understanding, taken away by the devil.	Unprotected, easily taken by the devil.
"Seeds fell on rocky places."	Receives the Word with joy, but lacks depth and stolen by trouble and persecution of the world.	"Walking on rocky places," = times of trouble, persecution, and lack of depth in the matter.
"Seeds fell on thorns."	The Word of God is heard, but choked by worries of life or the attraction of worldly riches.	Thorns = worries of life , distraction by worldly riches.
"Seeds on good soil."	Hears the Word, understands and becomes fruitful.	Well prepared for life expectancy, conducive for growth.

Benefits of a Parable Language

- Economy—a picture is worth a thousand words.
- It shows the essence—you apply the specifics to your situation; gives the principle so that the essence can be applicable at other times.

- A parable allows God to code messages for the dreamer.
- Is protected by hiding the promise from the enemy.
- Allows God to package and unfold His message according to the areas of priority.

The disciples came to Him and asked, "Why do You speak to the people in parables?" He replied, "The knowledge of the secrets of the kingdom of heaven has been given to you, but not to them. Whoever has will be given more, and he will have abundance. Whoever does not have, even what he has will be taken from him. This is why I speak to them in parables: 'Though seeing, they do not see; though hearing, they do not hear or understand' " (Matthew 13:10-13).

I spoke to the prophets, gave them many visions and told parables through them (Hosea 12:10).

- The mind speaks in the language of reason and concepts, but dreams speak in the language of riddles and parables.
- The language of pictures and symbols is universal and has no age barrier.
- Allows God to give the best possible picture or the truest perspective of the situation.
- A dream parable often shows the present condition and what will happen if we continue to go in the same direction.

*The proverbs (truths obscurely expressed, maxims, and **parables**) of Solomon son of David, king of Israel: That people may know skillful and godly wisdom and instruction, discern and comprehend the words of understanding and insight. Receive instruction in wise dealing and the discipline of wise thoughtfulness, righteousness, justice, and integrity. That prudence may be given to the simple, and knowledge, discretion, and discernment to the youth. The wise also will hear and increase in learning and the person of understanding will acquire skill and attain to sound counsel [so that he may be able to steer his course rightly]. That people may understand a proverb **[parable]** and a figure of speech or an enigma with its interpretation, and the words of the wise and their dark saying or riddles* (Proverbs 1:1-6 AMP, emphasis added).

CHAPTER 5

HOW TO USE THE DICTIONARY OF DREAM SYMBOLS

A seer receives in the language of symbols. However, in order to be relevant to the contemporary world, the seer should communicate the revelations with wisdom in language that people will understand. A seer should therefore be a student of the language of symbols and be able to communicate in simple terms with the people.

In general, when one sees a picture and switches to symbolic thinking, two questions should arise in the mind: What is the literal meaning of the picture? And what does the picture evoke? The answer to the first question will usually be the most obvious meaning for the symbol. In order to capture or broaden it to include the complete perspective of all the possible meanings, the second question must then be asked. This will help to explore the connotations and overtones in addition to the literal or most obvious meaning. If either of these two aspects is not well understood, the understanding of pictorial language is impoverished and not complete.

Example: The word *wife* is ordinarily understood to mean female, woman. This word also evokes some lateral thinking (connotations)—mother, home keeper, the Church, Bride of Christ.

Types of Symbol

A *metaphor* is a symbol with implied comparison (for example, the *tongue* as the pen of a ready writer; or *Jesus*, the Lion of the tribe of Judah). A *simile*, on the other hand, compares one thing to another and it makes the comparison explicit by using formula as "like" or "as." For example, "As the deer pants for water, so my soul pants for You." A *motif* is a pattern that appears in written text or a mental picture that has emerged from a written text. We allow the motif to develop wherever the Bible says, "Selah," i.e., pause and think.

Ezekiel—A Biblical Example

God described Ezekiel as the watchman to the house of Israel and He used extensive symbolism in most of His communications with the Prophet Ezekiel. Let us see how the above principles can help us understand the multiple dimensions to the symbolism in Ezekiel's vision of the valley of dry bones.

> *The hand of the Lord was upon me, and He brought me out by the Spirit of the Lord and set me in the middle of a valley; it was full of bones. He led me back and forth among them, and I saw a great many bones on the floor of the valley, bones that were very dry. He asked me, "Son of man, can these bones live?" I said, "O Sovereign Lord, You alone know." Then He said to me, "Prophesy to these bones and say to them, 'Dry bones, hear the word of the Lord! This is what the Sovereign Lord says to these bones: I will make breath enter you, and you will come to life. I will attach tendons to you and make flesh come upon you and cover you with skin; I will put breath in you, and you will come to life. Then you will know that I am the Lord.'" So I prophesied as I was commanded. And as I was prophesying, there was a noise, a rattling sound, and the bones came together, bone to bone. I looked, and tendons and flesh appeared on them and skin covered them, but there was no breath in them. Then He said to me, "Prophesy to the breath; prophesy, son of man, and say to it, 'This is what the Sovereign Lord says: Come from the four winds, O breath, and breathe into these slain, that they may live.'" So I prophesied as He commanded me, and breath entered them; they came to life and stood up on their feet—a vast army* (Ezekiel 37:1-10).

The interpretation given by God:

> *Then He said to me: "Son of man, these bones are the whole house of Israel. They say, 'Our bones are dried up and our hope is gone; we are cut off.' Therefore prophesy and say to them: 'This is what the Sovereign Lord says: O My people, I am going to open your graves and bring you up from them; I will bring you back to the land of Israel.*

Then you, My people, will know that I am the Lord, when I open your graves and bring you up from them. I will put My Spirit in you and you will live, and I will settle you in your own land. Then you will know that I the Lord have spoken, and I have done it, declares the Lord' " (Ezekiel 37:1-14).

The Anatomy of Ezekiel's Vision

SYMBOL	MEANING	THE POWER OF IMAGERY
A collection of dry bones littering a valley floor.	A state of hopelessness; extreme hardship; impossibility.	
Scattered.	Jews scattered in the nations.	
The bones (the hopeless situation) came together and assembled into skeletons (bone to his bones).	Coming together as predestined, each bone identified the exact skeleton to which it originally belonged.	Coming together of the Jews to a state of their own as prophesied.
As he observed flesh and skin grew on the skeleton.	This speaks of comfort and protection from God that will eventually emerge, particularly during the process.	
The bodies stayed dead, until a dramatic moment when God put breath into them.	Not filled with the spirit of God until the time appointed for this to happen.	After the restoration and recovery from the dead situation, the people remained spiritually dead. Their old souls needed to be renewed. The word "breath" also means spirit and the vision is reminiscent of Genesis 2:7 where God breathed life into the first man.

SYMBOL	MEANING	THE POWER OF IMAGERY
Come from the four winds.	The role of the four corners of the world in the eventual salvation of Israel.	God is saying that it would take a miracle to bring the remnants of Israel back together from many locations or nations where they are scattered. Israel will need an even greater miracle to be spiritually born-again with the spirit of God.
Vast army.	The eventual strength of the army of Israel, as it shall be like the army of the Lord.	

Using the Dictionary

This dictionary has been designed to assist the reader in broadening lateral thinking and to prevent or resist the tendency to become fixed on the meaning of a symbol. If you are fixed on the meaning of a symbol, you become limited in the benefits that can be obtained from a dream.

The following points are important to bear in mind when using the dictionary of symbols:

- Interpretation belongs to God. Therefore, attempting to use this dictionary without the help of the Holy Spirit is a futile exercise.

- This dictionary is not a carte blanche for dream interpretation.

- The true meaning of a symbol must be drawn within the context of each dream; do not be fixed on the meaning of a symbol as it could vary from dream to dream and from person to person.

- The Bible says that God expresses spiritual truth in spiritual words; the derived meaning for a symbol must therefore be largely dependent on the Word of God.

- The reader must bear in mind at all times that what is personally descriptive should not be taken as generally prescriptive. God deals with each one of us uniquely.

PART 2

DICTIONARY

of

DREAM SYMBOLS

ACID: Something that eats from within. Keeping offense or hatred, or malice.

See to it that no one misses the grace of God and that no bitter root grows up to cause trouble and defile many (Hebrews 12:15).

ADULTERY: Unfaithfulness regarding things of the Spirit or of the natural or actual adultery; lust for the pleasures of this world; sin.

The acts of the sinful nature are obvious: sexual immorality, impurity and debauchery; idolatry and witchcraft; hatred, discord, jealousy, fits of rage, selfish ambition, dissensions, factions (Galatians 5:19-20).

You adulterous people, don't you know that friendship with the world is hatred toward God? Anyone who chooses to be a friend of the world becomes an enemy of God (James 4:4).

AIRPLANE: A personal ministry or church, capable of moving in the Holy Spirit. Flowing in high spiritual power. Holy Spirit-powered ministry.

Crashing: The end of one phase, change of direction.

High: Fully powered in the Spirit.

Airplane
Crashing

Low: Only partially operative in the Spirit.

Soaring: Deep in the Spirit or moving in the deep things of God.

War plane: Call to intercessory ministry or spiritual warfare.

War Plane

AIRPORT: The ministry that sends out missionaries. High-powered spiritual church capable of equipping and sending out ministries. Preparation for ministry/provision or nourishment in readiness for service.

ALLIGATOR: Large-mouthed enemy. Verbal attacks.

Alligator

ALTAR: A place set apart for spiritual rituals or prayers/worship, whether good or bad.

David built an altar to the Lord there and sacrificed burnt offerings and fellowship offerings. Then the Lord answered

Altar

prayer in behalf of the land, and the plague on Israel was stopped (2 Samuel 24:25).

Then Noah built an altar to the Lord and, taking some of all the clean animals and clean birds, he sacrificed burnt offerings on it (Genesis 8:20).

There he built an altar, and he called the place El Bethel, because it was there that God revealed Himself to him when he was fleeing from his brother (Genesis 35:7).

Destroy completely all the places on the high mountains and on the hills and under every spreading tree where the nations you are dispossessing worship their gods. Break down their altars, smash their sacred stones and burn their Asherah poles in the fire; cut down the idols of their gods and wipe out their names from those places (Deuteronomy 12:2-3).

ANCHOR: The pillar that something or someone hangs on; something that hope is built on.

We have this hope as an anchor for the soul, firm and secure. It enters the inner sanctuary behind the curtain (Hebrews 6:19).

Anchor

ANKLES: Little faith, early stages.

As the man went eastward with a measuring line in his hand, he measured off a thousand cubits and then led me through water that was ankle-deep (Ezekiel 47:3).

ANOINT: Equipping with the Holy Spirit for service. The power of Holy Spirit to do something; sanctification; set apart for something.

Is any one of you sick? He should call the elders of the church to pray over him and anoint him with oil in the name of the Lord (James 5:14).

Also, anoint Jehu son of Nimshi king over Israel, and anoint Elisha son of Shaphat from Abel Meholah to succeed you as prophet (1 Kings 19:16).

ANT: Industrious, ability to plan ahead. Conscious of seasons of life. Unwanted guest.

Go to the ant, you sluggard; consider its ways and be wise! It has no commander, no overseer or ruler, yet it stores its provisions in summer and gathers its food at harvest (Proverbs 6:6-8).

Ants are creatures of little strength, yet they store up their food in the summer (Proverbs 30:25).

ANTIQUES: Something relating to the past. An inherited thing, whether good or bad.

This is what the Lord says: "Stand at the crossroads and look; ask for the ancient paths, ask where the good way is, and walk in it, and you will find rest for your souls." But you said, "We will not walk in it" (Jeremiah 6:16).

APPLES: Spiritual fruit, temptation; something precious like the apple of God's eyes.

When the woman saw that the fruit of the tree was good for food and pleasing to the eye, and also desirable for gaining wisdom, she took some and ate it. She also gave some to her husband, who was with her, and he ate it (Genesis 3:6).

Apple

In a desert land He found him, in a barren and howling waste. He shielded him and cared for him; He guarded him as the apple of His eye (Deuteronomy 32:10).

For this is what the Lord Almighty says: "After he has honored Me and has sent Me against the nations that have plundered you—for whoever touches you touches the apple of His eye (Zechariah 2:8).

ARK: Something relating to God's presence. Something of strength.

Place the cover on top of the ark and put in the ark the Testimony, which I will give you. There, above the cover between the two cherubim that are over the ark of the Testimony, I will meet with you and give you all my commands for the Israelites (Exodus 25:21-22).

Ark

ARM: Power and strength, whether good or bad.

But his bow remained steady, his strong arms stayed limber, because of the hand of the Mighty One of Jacob, because of the Shepherd, the Rock of Israel (Genesis 49:24).

Arm

Therefore, say to the Israelites: "I am the Lord, and I will bring you out from under the yoke of the Egyptians. I will free you from being slaves to them, and I will redeem you with an outstretched arm and with mighty acts of judgment (Exodus 6:6).

"With him is only the arm of flesh, but with us is the Lord our God to help us and to fight our battles." And the people gained confidence from what Hezekiah the king of Judah said (2 Chronicles 32:8).

Who has believed our message and to whom has the arm of the Lord been revealed? (Isaiah 53:1)

ARMIES: Spiritual warriors, whether good or bad.

ARMOR: Spiritual covering that protects against attacks. Divine protection. The truth of God.

Finally, be strong in the Lord and in His mighty power. Put on the full armor of God so that you can take your stand against the devil's schemes (Ephesians 6:10-11).

Armor

ARROWS: Powerful words, whether good or bad. Word of God or curses from the devil. Spiritual children. Good or bad intentions.

Sons are a heritage from the Lord, children a reward from Him. Like arrows in the hands of a warrior are sons born in one's youth (Psalm 127:3-4).

Arrows

They sharpen their tongues like swords and aim their words like deadly arrows (Psalm 64:3).

Like a club or a sword or a sharp arrow is the man who gives false testimony against his neighbor (Proverbs 25:18).

"Open the east window," he said, and he opened it. "Shoot!" Elisha said, and he shot. "The Lord's arrow of victory, the arrow of victory over Aram!" Elisha declared. "You will completely destroy the Arameans at Aphek" (2 Kings 13:17).

He made my mouth like a sharpened sword, in the shadow of His hand He hid me; He made me into a polished arrow and concealed me in His quiver (Isaiah 49:2).

ASHES: Signs of repentance or sorrow. To humble oneself. As a memorial.

Your maxims are proverbs of ashes; your defenses are defenses of clay (Job 13:12).

My ears had heard of you but now my eyes have seen you. Therefore I despise myself and repent in dust and ashes (Job 42:5-6).

Tamar put ashes on her head and tore the ornamented robe she was wearing. She put her hand on her head and went away, weeping aloud as she went (2 Samuel 13:19).

ATOM BOMB: Something capable of great destruction. Something of great suddenness or quick in occurring.

ATTIC: The mind-zone. Thought process. The spirit-realm. Memories/past issues/stored-up materials.

Atom Bomb

About noon the following day as they were on their journey and approaching the city, Peter went up on the roof to pray. He became hungry and wanted something to eat, and while the meal was being prepared, he fell into a trance. He saw heaven opened and something like a large sheet being let down to earth by its four corners (Acts 10:9-11).

AUTOGRAPH: Prominence or fame.

AUTUMN: Transition. The close of harvest season or about to enter difficult times. End of something and beginning of another.

They do not say to themselves, "Let us fear the Lord our God, who gives autumn and spring rains in season, who assures us of the regular weeks of harvest" (Jeremiah 5:24).

Autumn

AUTOBIKE: A Spirit-powered ministry that has either one-man or two-person involvement. Single-man ministry with a lot of exhibitionism.

Autobike

AUTOMOBILE: Means of getting to a destination or achieving the desired goal.

The chariots storm through the streets, rushing back and forth through the squares. They look like flaming torches; they dart about like lightning (Nahum 2:4).

Air-condition: If in good working condition, indicates adequate comfort despite prevailing situation; but if not working, indicates faulty provision for comfort.

Brakes: Slowing down; to stop; compelled to stop; hindrance.

Convertible: Capable of open-heaven ministration; revelatory ministry.

Driver-seat: Indicates leadership.

Engine: Holy Spirit power.

Four-wheel drive: A powerful ministry; ground breaking; capable of global influence.

Junkyard: Ministries that are abandoned or in need of repairs.

Rearview mirror: Looking back, focusing on things in the past; warning to look ahead; warning to watch your back.

Seatbelt: Something that ensures safety; fastened = prepared, prayers; unfastened = prayerlessness, carelessness.

Steering: The controlling and leading part.

Tires: Symbolic of the spiritual conditions of the ministry; flat = needing spiritual enabling, needing more prayers; full = powered by the Spirit.

Topless van: Not having adequate anointing for the occasion; vulnerable, transparent.

Van: Goods = delivering, group ministering.

Vehicle key: Authority in the ministry.

Wreck: Crashing, clash, end of one phase, change of direction. Danger. Contention or confrontation or offense.

AWAKENING: To be alert, watchfulness; to be stirred into action.

Then the Lord awoke as from sleep, as a man wakes from the stupor of wine (Psalm 78:65).

Awake, awake! Clothe yourself with strength, O arm of the Lord; awake, as in days gone by, as in generations of old. Was it not you who cut Rahab to pieces, who pierced that monster through? (Isaiah 51:9)

"Awake, O sword, against My shepherd, against the man who is close to Me!" declares the Lord Almighty. "Strike the shepherd, and the sheep will be scattered, and I will turn My hand against the little ones" (Zechariah 13:7).

AXE: The Word of God. To encourage by kind word. Issue that needs to be settled.

The ax is already at the root of the trees, and every tree that does not produce good fruit will be cut down and thrown into the fire (Matthew 3:10).

Axe

BABY: The beginning of something new. Beginning to be productive. New Christians. Something in its infancy or early stages.

Like newborn babies, crave pure spiritual milk, so that by it you may grow up in your salvation (1 Peter 2:2).

Brothers, I could not address you as spiritual but as worldly—mere infants in Christ. I gave you milk, not solid food, for you were not yet ready for it. Indeed, you are still not ready (1 Corinthians 3:1-2).

BACK: Pertaining to the past. Something behind or hidden. Out of view. Concealed thing.

> *Answer me, O Lord , answer me, so these people will know that You, O Lord, are God, and that You are turning their hearts back again* (1 Kings 18:37).

> *Let no one in the field go back to get his cloak* (Mark 13:16).

> *Jesus replied, "No one who puts his hand to the plow and looks back is fit for service in the kingdom of God"* (Luke 9:62).

BACKSIDE: Something in the past or behind the dreamer. Something concealed from view or understanding.

BADGER: Underground dwellers.

BAKER: One who instigates or originates something.

BAKING: Making provision for feeding people. Preparation for welfare ministry. God's provision.

BALANCES: Something reflecting both sides of the matter. Something waiting to tilt one way or the other. Judgment.

BALD HEAD: Lacking wisdom.

BALM: Healing, anointing; something to relieve pains, stress, or agony.

Balance

> *Is there no balm in Gilead? Is there no physician there? Why then is there no healing for the wound of My people?* (Jeremiah 8:22).

> *Babylon will suddenly fall and be broken. Wail over her! Get balm for her pain; perhaps she can be healed* (Jeremiah 51:8).

> *Judah and Israel traded with you; they exchanged wheat from Minnith and confections, honey, oil and balm for your wares* (Ezekiel 27:17).

BANK: Heavenly account. God's favor for a future season. A place of safety/security. A dependable place or source. God's provision.

> *Not that I am looking for a gift, but I am looking for what may be credited to your account* (Philippians 4:17).

> *But store up for yourselves treasures in heaven, where moth and rust do not destroy, and where thieves do not break in and steal* (Matthew 6:20).

BANNER, FLAG: The covering to which everyone belongs or is committed to. Something that brings unity, love, or purpose; a unifying object or circumstance. Victory.

Moses built an altar and called it The Lord is my Banner (Exodus 17:15).

Banner

BANQUET: God's provision. A full cup. Plentiful/affluence/abundance. Satisfaction. Blessing. Celebrations. Structured teaching of the Word of God.

He has taken me to the banquet hall, and his banner over me is love (Song of Solomon 2:4).

King Belshazzar gave a great banquet for a thousand of his nobles and drank wine with them....As they drank the wine, they praised the gods of gold and silver, of bronze, iron, wood and stone. Suddenly the fingers of a human hand appeared and wrote on the plaster of the wall, near the lampstand in the royal palace. The king watched the hand as it wrote (Daniel 5:1,4-5).

BAPTIZING: A change from the natural to the spiritual. Dying to self and expression of the new man.

He went into all the country around the Jordan, preaching a baptism of repentance for the forgiveness of sins (Luke 3:3).

We were therefore buried with Him through baptism into death in order that, just as Christ was raised from the dead through the glory of the Father, we too may live a new life (Romans 6:4).

Having been buried with Him in baptism and raised with Him through your faith in the power of God, who raised Him from the dead (Colossians 2:12).

BARBERSHOP: Time, place, period of changing beliefs or customs or habits. A church where these can take place. Depending on the emphasis, either a place of vanity or correction.

Barbershop

BARENESS: Unproductive, difficult time or period.

BARN: A place of provision. A church. Stored spiritual wealth.

Let both grow together until the harvest. At that time I will tell the harvesters: First collect the weeds and tie them in

Barn

bundles to be burned; then gather the wheat and bring it into my barn (Matthew 13:30).

Is there yet any seed left in the barn? Until now, the vine and the fig tree, the pomegranate and the olive tree have not borne fruit. "From this day on I will bless you" (Haggai 2:19).

BASEMENT: The unseen part of something. Storage zone. Related to the foundation. Hidden. Bloodline related issue.

BASKET: A measure of God's provision. A measure of judgment.

This is what the Sovereign Lord showed me: a basket of ripe fruit. "What do you see, Amos?" He asked. "A basket of ripe fruit," I answered. Then the Lord said to me, "The time is ripe for My people Israel; I will spare them no longer" (Amos 8:1-2).

Basket

Then the angel who was speaking to me came forward and said to me, "Look up and see what this is that is appearing." I asked, "What is it?" He replied, "It is a measuring basket." And he added, "This is the iniquity of the people throughout the land." Then the cover of lead was raised, and there in the basket sat a woman! He said, "This is wickedness," and he pushed her back into the basket and pushed the lead cover down over its mouth. Then I looked up—and there before me were two women, with the wind in their wings! They had wings like those of a stork, and they lifted up the basket between heaven and earth. "Where are they taking the basket?" I asked the angel who was speaking to me. He replied, "To the country of Babylonia to build a house for it. When it is ready, the basket will be set there in its place" (Zechariah 5:5-11).

BAT: Creature of darkness. Satanic instrument, related to witchcraft. A nighttime creature. Could represent association with the dark side of life.

Bat

BATHING: What you do on the outside or outwardly to prevent unclean or unholy attitude. Outward repentance.

BATHROOM: A period of cleansing/entering a time of repentance. A place of voluntary nakedness or facing reality in individual life.

Bathing

BEAM: Power or illumination coming from God or the heavenly. A time of exposure. A time of spotlight.

BEAR: Danger, wicked person or spirit, vindictiveness. Evil; something that is after what you possess.

Bear

> *But David said to Saul, "Your servant has been keeping his father's sheep. When a lion or a bear came and carried off a sheep from the flock, I went after it, struck it and rescued the sheep from its mouth. When it turned on me, I seized it by its hair, struck it and killed it. Your servant has killed both the lion and the bear; this uncircumcised Philistine will be like one of them, because he has defied the armies of the living God. The Lord who delivered me from the paw of the lion and the paw of the bear will deliver me from the hand of this Philistine." Saul said to David, "Go, and the Lord be with you"* (1 Samuel 17:34-37).

> *You know your father and his men; they are fighters, and as fierce as a wild bear robbed of her cubs. Besides, your father is an experienced fighter; he will not spend the night with the troops* (2 Samuel 17:8).

> *It will be as though a man fled from a lion only to meet a bear, as though he entered his house and rested his hand on the wall only to have a snake bite him* (Amos 5:19).

BEARD: To have respect for those in authority.

Messing: Insanity.

Trimmed: Sane.

BEAUTY SHOP: A place of preparation with emphasis on outward appearance, tending towards vanity.

BED: Revelations, rest, contentment. Becoming relaxed or lax.

Bed

BEDROOM: A place of intimacy. A place of rest, sleep, or dreams. A place of covenant, a place of revelation.

BEES: That which makes offensive noise. More noisy than effective. A double-edged situation capable of going bad or producing sweetness. Stinging words, gossip.

> *Some time later, when he went back to marry her, he turned aside to look at the lion's carcass. In it was a swarm of bees and some honey* (Judges 14:8).

BELLS: Call to attention or action. To bring to alertness. To say it loudly; public warning.

BELLY: Feelings, desires, spiritual well-being, sentiment.

BICYCLE: A ministry depending on much human effort. One-man ministry.

Bell

BINOCULARS: Looking ahead, looking into the future. Prophetic ministry.

BIRD: Symbol of leader, evil or good at different levels. Agents of authority.

Binoculars

> *Dove*: Holy Spirit. Holy Spirit—peace; a seal of approval from Heaven.

> *Eagle*: Symbol of personality or spirit capable of soaring in the Spirit. Good focus/swiftness; powerful. A prophet of God. The nation of America.

> *Owl*: An evil eye that monitors; spirit of craftiness.

> *Raven*: Symbol of unclean spirit.

> *Sparrow*: Divine provision and food. Symbol of God's desire to provide for us.

Owl

> *Vulture*: Evil spirit, opportunistic person. Night creature or something that preys on "dead things" (human weaknesses). Unclean spirit. A loner.

> *Feathers*: A protective covering, a shield or instrument for flying or moving in the spirit.

> *Wings*: A place of refuge. God's presence. Safety/something that provides escape from danger.

> *Fowler*: A person or spirit that entraps. Fowler's net.

BLACK: Lack, famine. Evil, demonic spirit. Darkness.

> *May darkness and deep shadow claim it once more; may a cloud settle over it; may blackness overwhelm its light* (Job 3:5).

> *They are wild waves of the sea, foaming up their shame; wandering stars, for whom blackest darkness has been reserved forever* (Jude 1:13).

> *I clothe the sky with darkness and make sackcloth its covering* (Isaiah 50:3).

BLEEDING: Hurting. To loose spiritually. Verbal accusation. Traumatic.

BLIND: Lack of understanding, ignorance. Not able to see into the spirit world.

BLOOD: Atonement, to appease. Something that testifies.

BLOOD TRANSFUSION: Getting new life, rescuing situation.

BLUE: Heaven-related visitation from God or of the Holy Spirit. Spiritual.

BOAT: A ministry that is capable of influencing many people.

Boat

BODY ODOR: Unclean spirit, after effect of fleshy actions.

BONES: The substance of something. The main issue. Long lasting.

> *Skeleton*: Something without flesh/substance. Something without details.

Bone

BOOK: Gaining understanding/knowledge. Scriptures. Revelation. Promise from God. Message from the title of the book.

BOTTLE: Something relating to the body as the container of anointing.

Book

BOW, ARROW OR GUN: Source from which attacks come. The power of a nation or person. Verbal attacks. The tongue.

> *But his bow remained steady, his strong arms stayed limber, because of the hand of the Mighty One of Jacob, because of the Shepherd, the Rock of Israel (Genesis 49:24).*
>
> *"They make ready their tongue like a bow, to shoot lies; it is not by truth that they triumph in the land. They go from one sin to another; they do not acknowledge Me," declares the Lord (Jeremiah 9:3).*
>
> *This is what the Lord Almighty says: "See, I will break the bow of Elam, the mainstay of their might" (Jeremiah 49:35).*

Bow

BOWL: A measure of something.

> *His offering was one silver plate weighing a hundred and thirty shekels, and one silver sprinkling bowl weighing seventy shekels, both*

according to the sanctuary shekel, each filled with fine flour mixed with oil as a grain offering (Numbers 7:13).

You drink wine by the bowlful and use the finest lotions, but you do not grieve over the ruin of Joseph (Amos 6:6).

And the Lord Almighty will shield them. They will destroy and overcome with slingstones. They will drink and roar as with wine; they will be full like a bowl used for sprinkling the corners of the altar (Zechariah 9:15).

And that is what happened. Gideon rose early the next day; he squeezed the fleece and wrung out the dew—a bowlful of water (Judges 6:38).

BRACELET: Pertaining to pride. Valuable but of the world. Identity if it has a name.

Bracelet

BRANCHES: God's people, churches. Church split.

I am the vine; you are the branches. If a man remains in Me and I in him, he will bear much fruit; apart from Me you can do nothing (John 15:5).

I am the true vine, and My Father is the gardener. He cuts off every branch in Me that bears no fruit, while every branch that does bear fruit He prunes so that it will be even more fruitful (John 15:1-2).

BRASS: Hardness, hard covering. Judgment/captivity/hard to break out from. Strength. Negative stronghold.

Do I have the strength of stone? Is my flesh bronze [brass]? (Job 6:12)

The sky over your head will be bronze [brass], the ground beneath you iron (Deuteronomy 28:23).

They killed the sons of Zedekiah before his eyes. Then they put out his eyes, bound him with bronze [brass] shackles and took him to Babylon (2 Kings 25:7).

I will break down your stubborn pride and make the sky above you like iron and the ground beneath you like bronze (Leviticus 26:19).

BREAD: Jesus Christ; Bread of life, Word of God, source of nourishment, God's provision.

Bread

Then she arose with her daughters-in-law that she might return from the country of Moab, for she had heard in the country of Moab that the Lord had visited His people by giving them bread (Ruth 1:6 NKJ).

At this the Jews began to grumble about Him because He said, "I am the bread that came down from heaven" (John 6:41).

A man ought to examine himself before he eats of the bread and drinks of the cup (1 Corinthians 11:28).

Give us today our daily bread (Matthew 6:11).

Fresh: New word from God.

Moldy: Something that is not new. Unclean.

Unleavened: Showing lack of sin.

BREAST: Source of milk for new Christians. Object of enticement. Source of sustenance.

Because of your father's God, who helps you, because of the Almighty, who blesses you with blessings of the heavens above, blessings of the deep that lies below, blessings of the breast and womb (Genesis 49:25).

Why were there knees to receive me and breasts that I might be nursed? (Job 3:12)

A loving doe, a graceful deer—may her breasts satisfy you always, may you ever be captivated by her love (Proverbs 5:19).

BREASTPLATE: God's protective shield. Covering or the anointing which covers one. Preparing to give judgment. Protective of vital human organs or issues.

He put on righteousness as his breastplate, and the helmet of salvation on his head; he put on the garments of vengeance and wrapped himself in zeal as in a cloak (Isaiah 59:17).

He placed the breastpiece on him and put the Urim and Thummim in the breastpiece (Leviticus 8:8).

Stand firm then, with the belt of truth buckled around your waist, with the breastplate of righteousness in place (Ephesians 6:14).

BREATH: Spirit of man. Breath of life. Sign of life. Revive to life.

The Lord God formed the man from the dust of the ground and breathed into his nostrils the breath of life, and the man became a living being (Genesis 2:7).

His breath sets coals ablaze, and flames dart from his mouth (Job 41:21).

Topheth has long been prepared; it has been made ready for the king. Its fire pit has been made deep and wide, with an abundance of fire and wood; the breath of the Lord, like a stream of burning sulphur, sets it ablaze (Isaiah 30:33).

Then he said to me, "Prophesy to the breath; prophesy, son of man, and say to it, 'This is what the Sovereign Lord says: Come from the four winds, O breath, and breathe into these slain, that they may live'" (Ezekiel 37:9).

BRICK: Something that is manmade; designed to be durable. Personality building.

They said to each other, "Come, let's make bricks and bake them thoroughly." They used brick instead of stone, and tar for mortar (Genesis 11:3).

The bricks have fallen down, but we will rebuild with dressed stone; the fig trees have been felled, but we will replace them with cedars (Isaiah 9:10).

A people who continually provoke Me to My very face, offering sacrifices in gardens and burning incense on altars of brick (Isaiah 65:3).

BRIDE: The Church relationship to Jesus. Special to Jesus. Covenant or relationship.

"Lift up your eyes and look around; all your sons gather and come to you. As surely as I live," declares the Lord, "you will wear them all as ornaments; you will put them on, like a bride" (Isaiah 49:18).

Bride

The bride belongs to the bridegroom. The friend who attends the bridegroom waits and listens for him, and is full of joy when he hears the bridegroom's voice. That joy is mine, and it is now complete (John 3:29).

One of the seven angels who had the seven bowls full of the seven last plagues came and said to me, "Come, I will show you the bride, the wife of the Lamb" (Revelation 21:9).

BRIDGE: Something that takes you across an obstacle, e.g. faith. The connection between two things/circumstances. Something that holds you up in times of difficulty.

Bridge

BRIDLE: Put control over, e.g. self-control over the use of the tongue. Something imposed by some higher authority to effect control—good or bad.

A whip for the horse, a bridle for the donkey, and a rod for the fool's back (Proverbs 26:3 NKJ).

If anyone among you thinks he is religious, and does not bridle his tongue but deceives his own heart, this one's religion is useless (James 1:26 NKJ).

I said, "I will watch my ways and keep my tongue from sin; I will put a muzzle [bridle] *on my mouth as long as the wicked are in my presence"* (Psalm 39:1).

Because your rage against Me and your tumult have come up to My ears, therefore I will put My hook in your nose and My bridle in your lips, and I will turn you back by the way which you came (Isaiah 37:29 NKJ).

BRIERS: Something "wild and thorny" that needs to be trimmed. Something uncultivated or false.

BRIGHTNESS: Presence of God. Revelation. Solution. End of difficult period.

I looked, and I saw a figure like that of a man. From what appeared to be his waist down he was like fire, and from there up his appearance was as bright as glowing metal (Ezekiel 8:2).

Those who are wise will shine like the brightness of the heavens, and those who lead many to righteousness, like the stars for ever and ever (Daniel 12:3).

You looked, O king, and there before you stood a large statue—an enormous, dazzling statue, awesome in appearance (Daniel 2:31).

The Son is the radiance (brightness) of God's glory and the exact representation of His being, sustaining all things by His powerful word. After He had provided purification for sins, He sat down at the right hand of the Majesty in heaven (Hebrews 1:3).

BRIMSTONE: Judgment of God. Punishment. Trail period.

BROKEN: Loss of strength, authority, or influence. Open. Heart, wounded.

Like a city whose walls are broken down is a man who lacks self-control (Proverbs 25:28).

I will seek what was lost and bring back what was driven away, bind up the broken and strengthen what was sick; but I will destroy the fat and the strong, and feed them in judgment (Ezekiel 34:16 NKJ).

BROOK: A provision of God. Something that brings refreshment, wisdom, prosperity from God. If dirty, means corrupted or contaminated. A source of defense.

Brook

The rivers will turn foul; the brooks of defense will be emptied and dried up; the reeds and rushes will wither (Isaiah 19:6 NKJ).

Get away from here and turn eastward, and hide by the Brook Cherith, which flows into the Jordan. And it will be that you shall drink from the brook, and I have commanded the ravens to feed you there (1 Kings 17:3-4 NKJ).

My brothers have dealt deceitfully like a brook, like the streams of the brooks that pass away (Job 6:15 NKJ).

BROOM: Something, or in the process of, getting rid of sins. Symbol of witchcraft.

Broom

BROTHER: Christian brother (spiritual brother). Your brother. Someone with similar qualities.

Whoever does God's will is my brother and sister and mother (Mark 3:35).

BROTHER-IN-LAW: Same as a brother but under special obligation. Spiritual brother without in-depth love. A person of another church who is also Christian. Actual brother-in-law. Someone with similar qualities.

BROWN/TAN: Life; change of season; born again.

BRUISE: Event or circumstance that leaves a hurt feeling with one. In need for healing. Suffering of Jesus on our behalf.

This is what the Lord says: "Your wound is incurable, your injury (bruise) beyond healing" (Jeremiah 30:12).

But He was wounded for our transgressions, He was bruised for our iniquities; the chastisement for our peace was upon Him, and by His stripes we are healed (Isaiah 53:5 NKJ).

BUCKET: A measure of something. Used for service. Supplies life.

Bucket

Surely the nations are like a drop in a bucket; they are regarded as dust on the scales; he weighs the islands as though they were fine dust (Isaiah 40:15).

Water will flow from their buckets; their seed will have abundant water. Their king will be greater than Agag; their kingdom will be exalted (Numbers 24:7).

BUILDING: Symbolic of the spiritual and emotional being of the place, person, or church. Life of the person, church, or office.

And I tell you that you are Peter, and on this rock I will build My church, and the gates of Hades will not overcome it (Matthew 16:18).

He is like a man building a house, who dug down deep and laid the foundation on rock. When a flood came, the torrent struck that house but could not shake it, because it was well built (Luke 6:48).

Therefore everyone who hears these words of Mine and puts them into practice is like a wise man who built his house on the rock. The rain came down, the streams rose, and the winds blew and beat against that house; yet it did not fall, because it had its foundation on the rock. But everyone who hears these words of Mine and does not put them into practice is like a foolish man who built his house on sand (Matthew 7:24-26).

BULL: Threatening situation. Warfare. Opposition. A source of economy.

BUNDLE: Measure of harvest. Grouping for judgment or reward. Fullness.

Bull

Then it happened as they emptied their sacks, that surprisingly each man's bundle of money was in his sack; and when they and their father saw the bundles of money, they were afraid (Genesis 42:35 NKJ).

Even though someone is pursuing you to take your life, the life of my master will be bound securely in the bundle of the living by the Lord your God. But the lives of your enemies He will hurl away as from the pocket of a sling (1 Samuel 25:29).

BURIAL: Memorial to mark the end of something.

Uzziah rested with his fathers and was buried near them in a field for burial that belonged to the kings, for people said, "He had leprosy." And Jotham his son succeeded him as king (2 Chronicles 26:23).

He will have the burial of a donkey—dragged away and thrown outside the gates of Jerusalem (Jeremiah 22:19).

When she poured this perfume on My body, she did it to prepare Me for burial (Matthew 26:12).

BURIED: A permanent end to something.

We were therefore buried with Him through baptism into death in order that, just as Christ was raised from the dead through the glory of the Father, we too may live a new life (Romans 6:4).

Having been buried with Him in baptism and raised with Him through your faith in the power of God, who raised Him from the dead (Colossians 2:12).

BURN: To consume. To heat up or strip up. To set aflame. To kindle. Sign of fervency.

Now the people complained about their hardships in the hearing of the Lord, and when He heard them His anger was aroused. Then fire from the Lord burned among them and consumed some of the outskirts of the camp (Numbers 11:1).

Burn

I will enslave you to your enemies in a land you do not know, for My anger will kindle a fire that will burn against you (Jeremiah 15:14).

Command the Israelites to bring you clear oil of pressed olives for the light so that the lamps may be kept burning (Exodus 27:20).

BUS: A big ministry.

School bus: A teaching ministry.

Bus

BUTTER: Something that brings soothing, smooth words. Encouragement.

He will eat curds [butter] and honey when he knows enough to reject the wrong and choose the right (Isaiah 7:15).

His speech is smooth as butter, yet war is in his heart; his words are more soothing than oil, yet they are drawn swords (Psalm 55:21).

BUY: To prepare, take, acquire, or obtain something good or bad.

Fields will be bought for silver, and deeds will be signed, sealed and witnessed in the territory of Benjamin, in the villages around Jerusalem, in the towns of Judah and in the towns of the hill country, of the western foothills and of the Negev, because I will restore their fortunes, declares the Lord (Jeremiah 32:44).

Buy the truth and do not sell it; get wisdom, discipline and understanding (Proverbs 23:23).

For a hundred pieces of silver, he bought from the sons of Hamor, the father of Shechem, the plot of ground where he pitched his tent (Genesis 33:19).

CAFETERIA: A place or period of spiritual nourishment/good or bad. A church. Structural teaching of the Word of God. Celebration.

CAGE: To restrict. Limited mobility. Negatively—captivity. Positively—to guard or watch.

Cage

Like cages full of birds, their houses are full of deceit; they have become rich and powerful (Jeremiah 5:27).

CAKE, BREAD: Provisions from Heaven. Nourishment from God.

Cake

The people went around gathering it, and then ground it in a handmill or crushed it in a mortar. They cooked it in a pot or made it into cakes. And it tasted like something made with olive oil (Numbers 11:8).

CALF: A young cow or bull. Increase in prosperity.

CAMEL: Having a servant heart. Capable of bearing other people's burdens. Intercessory spirit.

CAMP: Temporary settlement; a transit situation. Something intended for traveling or for temporary residence, not permanent building.

Jacob also went on his way, and the angels of God met him. When Jacob saw them, he said, "This is the camp of God!" So he named that place Mahanaim (Genesis 32:1-2).

They left the Red Sea and camped in the Desert of Sin. They left the Desert of Sin and camped at Dophkah. They left Dophkah and camped at Alush. They left Alush and camped at Rephidim, where there was no water for the people to drink. They left Rephidim and camped in the Desert of Sinai. They left the Desert of Sinai and camped at Kibroth Hattaavah. They left Kibroth Hattaavah and camped at Hazeroth. They left Hazeroth and camped at Rithmah (Numbers 33:11-18).

CANDLE: Word of God.

The lamp of the Lord searches the spirit of a man; it searches out his inmost being (Proverbs 20:27).

Candle

At that time I will search Jerusalem with lamps and punish those who are complacent, who are like wine left on its dregs, who think, "The Lord will do nothing, either good or bad" (Zephaniah 1:12).

Lamp and electricity: Symbolic of man's spirit. If not lit, it could mean lack of God's presence. (Jesus is also source of light.) Conscience.

CANDLESTICK: People who carry the light of God. The lamp stand, Spirit of God. Church.

CARPENTER: Jesus. Someone who makes or amends things. A preacher.

CAT: A personal pet. Deceptive situation/person. Something or a person who is self-willed. Not a teachable spirit. A sneaky, crafty, and deceptive spirit. Witchcraft, waiting to attack—a precious habit that could be dangerous.

Cat

CAVE: Safe hiding place. Secret place of encountering God.

CHAIN: Symbolic of bondage or captivity. To be bound in the spirit or in the natural.

Chain

CHAIR: Authority over something; coming to position of authority. Throne of God.

CHANNEL: A way out. A process of time. Difficult period leading to the next stage.

Chair

CHASE: Cause to flee. Get rid of something. To pursue. To go after something.

CHEQUE: The seal of promise. Promise that is guaranteed.

CHEEK: Vulnerable part, beauty.

CHEESE: To comfort. To soothe.

Cheese

CHEETAH: Unclean spirit.

CHEW: To meditate. To ruminate. To cut off.

Cheetah

CHICKEN: An evangelist. Gifting, caring spirit. Gathering.

O Jerusalem, Jerusalem, you who kill the prophets and stone those sent to you, how often I have longed to gather your children together, as a hen gathers her chicks under her wings, but you were not willing (Matthew 23:37, Luke 13:34).

Roaster: Boasting.

Chick: Defenseless.

CHILDHOOD home: Influence from the distant past, good or bad.

CHOKING: Biting more than you can chew. Too fast, too much in the wrong way.

CHRISTMAS: New thing in Christ. Tradition of men. Spiritual gift. Season of gifts/love. A period of joy and humanitarianism.

CIRCLE, RING/ROUND: Something endless; signifies agreement or covenant. Hunting, if making a circle. Relating to the universe.

He sits enthroned above the circle of the earth, and its people are like grasshoppers. He stretches out the heavens like a canopy, and spreads them out like a tent to live in (Isaiah 40:22).

CIRCUMCISION: Cutting off fleshy things/coming to liberty. Covenanting with God. Blood relationship. New levels of spiritual walk—born again.

You are to undergo circumcision, and it will be the sign of the covenant between Me and you (Genesis 17:11).

Circumcise yourselves to the Lord, circumcise your hearts, you men of Judah and people of Jerusalem, or My wrath will break out and burn like fire because of the evil you have done—burn with no one to quench it (Jeremiah 4:4).

Then He gave Abraham the covenant of circumcision. And Abraham became the father of Isaac and circumcised him eight days after his birth. Later Isaac became the father of Jacob, and Jacob became the father of the twelve patriarchs (Acts 7:8).

CITY: The makeup of the person. All that has been input into the person or people. The city or what the city is known for. Group, church.

City

CLASSROOM: A time of spiritual preparation. A person with a gifting to teach others.

CLAY: Something that refers to frailty of man. Delicate and fragile. Not secure.

> *I am just like you before God; I too have been taken from clay* (Job 33:6).
> *Its legs of iron, its feet partly of iron and partly of baked clay. While you were watching, a rock was cut out, but not by human hands. It struck the statue on its feet of iron and clay and smashed them....As the toes were partly iron and partly clay, so this kingdom will be partly strong and partly brittle* (Daniel 2:33-34,42).

CLEAN: To make holy, purity. To make righteous. To make ready and acceptable.

CLEANSE: To put something right. To put away what is bad.

CLEAR: To bring light to the situation. To bring understanding. To be set free from something.

CLOCK: Timing is important in the situation. The time to do it is revealed. May refer to Bible passages. Running out of time.

Clock

CLOSE: To shut up, to keep silent or to be hedged or walled up.

> *For the Lord has poured out on you the spirit of deep sleep, and has closed your eyes, namely, the prophets; and He has covered your heads, namely, the seers* (Isaiah 29:10 NKJ).
> *For this people's heart has become calloused; they hardly hear with their ears, and they have closed their eyes. Otherwise they might see with their eyes, hear with their ears, understand with their hearts and turn, and I would heal them* (Matthew 13:15).

CLOSET: Hidden, confidential, personal, or exclusive. A place of prayer. A place of fellowship with God.

> *Gather the people, consecrate the assembly; bring together the elders, gather the children, those nursing at the breast. Let the bridegroom leave his room and the bride her chamber* [closet] (Joel 2:16).
> *But when you pray, go into your room* [closet], *close the door and pray to your Father, who is unseen. Then your Father, who sees what is done in secret, will reward you* (Matthew 6:6).
> *What you have said in the dark will be heard in the daylight, and what you have whispered in the ear in the inner rooms* [closet] *will be proclaimed from the roofs* (Luke 12:3).

CLOTHING: Covering, whether pure or impure. Your standing or authority in a situation. Covering, God is providing us with.

Tearing clothes: Signifies grief, sorrow.

CLOUDS: Heavenly manifestation; glory presence of God. Dark time of travel, fear, trouble, or storms of life.

Clouds

By day the Lord went ahead of them in a pillar of cloud to guide them on their way and by night in a pillar of fire to give them light, so that they could travel by day or night (Exodus 13:21).

The Lord said to Moses: "Tell your brother Aaron not to come whenever he chooses into the Most Holy Place behind the curtain in front of the atonement cover on the ark, or else he will die, because I appear in the cloud over the atonement cover (Leviticus 16:2).

At that time the sign of the Son of Man will appear in the sky, and all the nations of the earth will mourn. They will see the Son of Man coming on the clouds of the sky, with power and great glory (Matthew 24:30).

Dark clouds: A time of storm.

White clouds: Glory of God.

CLOWN: Not a serious person. Not taking God seriously. Childish.

Clown

COAT: Protective, covering, mantle.

The Lord God made garments [coat] of skin for Adam and his wife and clothed them (Genesis 3:21).

He is to put on the sacred linen tunic, with linen undergarments next to his body; he is to tie the linen sash around him and put on the linen turban. These are sacred garments [coats]; so he must bathe himself with water before he puts them on (Leviticus 16:4).

Take the garments [coats] and dress Aaron with the tunic, the robe of the ephod, the ephod itself and the breastpiece. Fasten the ephod on him by its skillfully woven waistband (Exodus 29:5).

Clean: Righteousness.

Dirty: Not righteous, unclean.

COLLEGE: Promotion in the Spirit. Pertaining to the equipping season.

COLUMNS: Spirit of control and manipulation or obsessive orderliness.

CONCEIVE: In process of preparation. To add. To multiply.

CONGREGATION: An appointed meeting. An assembly. Called together.

CORD: Something that holds things together. Enhances unity/love.

COUCH: Rest, relaxation, peace.

Couch

COUNTRYSIDE: A time of peace/tranquillity. A potential that is yet unexplored.

COURTHOUSE: Time of being judged or persecution; trial.

COW: Food/source of enrichment. Potential source of sin.

CRAWLING: Humility or to be humiliated.

CROOKED: Distorted, not straight.

> *Every valley shall be raised up, every mountain and hill made low; the rough ground* [crooked] *shall become level* [straight]*, the rugged places a plain* (Isaiah 40:4).

> *But those who turn to crooked ways the Lord will banish with the evildoers. Peace be upon Israel* (Psalm 125:5).

CROSSING STREET: Changing perspectivė.

CROSSROADS: Vital choice to make or change in position. Options.

Crossing street

CROWN: Symbol of authority. Seal of power. Jesus Christ. To reign. To be honored.

Crown

CRYING: Actual crying. A period of grief, outburst of sadness. Intense emotional expression.

CULTURAL CLOTHES: Call to nation.

CUP: Your portion in life, provision or responsibility.

CYMBALS: Instrument to praise God with. Could be used without genuine love.

Cup

DAM: The power of unity or gathering resources. Obstacle to flow. Reserve sustenance. Stillness.

DANCING, WORSHIP: Worshipping something—God or idol. A time of joy or rejoicing.

Dam

DARKNESS: Lack of light. Without spiritual direction.

DAUGHTER: Gift of God. Ministry that is your child in the Spirit. The child herself. Someone with similar qualities.

DAYTIME: The opportune time. A time of light. Season of good deeds. Season when things are revealed or understanding is gained.

DEAF: Not spiritually attentive. Not paying attention.

DEATH: What the Bible says more frequently about death is dying to self. Some measure of dying to self in an area. Separation from things of evil; actual physical death. The end of life on earth. Death is also overcoming the work of the flesh to resume communion with God.

DEER: Spiritual longing. Symbol of hunger for the things of God. Ability to take great strides. Grace. Divine enabling.

Deer

> *As the deer pants for streams of water, so my soul pants for You, O God. My soul thirsts for God, for the living God. When can I go and meet with God?* (Psalm 42:1-2)

> *A loving doe, a graceful deer—may her breasts satisfy you always, may you ever be captivated by her love* (Proverbs 5:19).

> *The Sovereign Lord is my strength; He makes my feet like the feet of a deer, He enables me to go on the heights. For the director of music. On my stringed instruments* (Habakkuk 3:19).

DEN: Busy doing the wrong thing.

DESERT: Training, lack or testing. A place of reliance on God.

Desert

DEW: Blessings. Condensed, moisturised air formed in drops during still, cloudless night indicates divine blessing on the earth. The Word of God.

> *May God give you of heaven's dew and of earth's richness—an abundance of grain and new wine* (Genesis 27:28).

> *It is as if the dew of Hermon were falling on Mount Zion. For there the Lord bestows His blessing, even life forevermore* (Psalm 133:3).

> *Let my teaching fall like rain and my words descend like dew, like showers on new grass, like abundant rain on tender plants* (Deuteronomy 32:2).

> *Therefore, because of you the heavens have withheld their dew and the earth its crops* (Haggai 1:10).

DIAMOND: Something to engrave with, something hard, and something that is sharp at cutting. Diamond as a pen nib. Something valuable.

Diamond

DIFFICULT WALKING: Difficult times of life. Facing opposition.

DINING ROOM: Feeding on the Word of God. A place of spiritual food. Table of the Lord.

DINOSAUR: Something in the distant past. Something big and terrible but something God has dealt with.

Dinosaur

DIRTY CLOTH: False doctrine. Of a sinful nature.

> *Now Joshua was dressed in filthy clothes as he stood before the angel. The angel said to those who were standing before him, "Take off his filthy clothes." Then he said to Joshua, "See, I have taken away your sin, and I will put rich garments on you." Then I said, "Put a clean turban on his head." So they put a clean turban on his head and clothed him, while the angel of the Lord stood by* (Zechariah 3:3-5).

DIRTY/DRY: Not pure spiritual things.

DIRTY/NEGLECTED: A place in need of attention.

DISEASE: Emotional upset. Bondage from the devil.

DITCH: Deception, a trap; fleshy desire.

DOCTOR: Jesus—the healer. A person with healing anointing. Someone with caring service, minister. Symbol of healing anointing.

DOG: A gift that could be harnessed to do good, but should not be too trusted. Could be versatile in function but unpredictable. Man's best friend. A pet sin.

DONKEY: An enduring spirit, useable by the Lord. A spirit that God could use if surrendered to Him.

DOOR: An opening. Jesus Christ. The way, a possibility, grace. Something to do with Jesus.

> *Set a guard over my mouth, O Lord; keep watch over the door of my lips* (Psalm 141:3).

Door

Therefore Jesus said again, "I tell you the truth, I am the gate [door] for the sheep. All who ever came before Me were thieves and robbers, but the sheep did not listen to them. I am the gate [door]; whoever enters through Me will be saved. He will come in and go out, and find pasture (John 10:7-9).

After this I looked, and there before me was a door standing open in heaven. And the voice I had first heard speaking to me like a trumpet said, "Come up here, and I will show you what must take place after this" (Revelation 4:1).

DOWN: Spiritual descent/backslide. Falling away. Humiliation. Failure.

DRAGON: Satan. High demonic spirit. Great level of wickedness. Antichrist.

Then another sign appeared in heaven: an enormous red dragon with seven heads and ten horns and seven crowns on his heads (Revelation 12:3).

Dragon

The great dragon was hurled down—that ancient serpent called the devil, or satan, who leads the whole world astray. He was hurled to the earth, and his angels with him (Revelation 12:9).

DRAWING: Conceptualization.

Artist's paint: A means or method of illustration. To be fluent in expression.

Paint: Doctrine, truth, or deception.

DREAMING: Deeply spiritual message. A futuristic message.

DRINKING: Receiving from the spiritual realm, good or bad. Receiving your portion in life. Bearing your cross.

DRIVER: The one in command or control. The one that makes the decisions.

DRIVING IN REVERSE: Not going in correct direction with anointing.

DROUGHT: A period of lack without God.

DROWNING: Overcome by situation leading to depression. Overwhelmed to the point of self-pity.

DRUGS: Medication. Illicit drugs = counterfeit anointing.

DRUNKARD: Influenced by counterfeit source of anointing. Self-indulgence error. Uncontrolled lust.

Drugs

DUST: Temporary nature of humanity. Frailty of man. Curse. Numerous. Humiliation.

> *The Lord God formed the man from the dust of the ground and breathed into his nostrils the breath of life, and the man became a living being* (Genesis 2:7).

> *Your descendants will be like the dust of the earth, and you will spread out to the west and to the east, to the north and to the south. All peoples on earth will be blessed through you and your offspring* (Genesis 28:14).

> *Shake off your dust; rise up, sit enthroned, O Jerusalem. Free yourself from the chains on your neck, O captive Daughter of Zion* (Isaiah 52:2).

DYNAMITE: Holy Spirit "dynamos"—power/great spiritual power, good or bad.

EAR: Symbolic of the prophet—not the seer. Hearing spiritual things that either build up or tear down. Lack of hearing or need to be paying more attention.

Dynamite

EARTHQUAKE: Sudden release of great power. Judgment. Ground-shaking changes. Great shock. A time of trial. Release from prison.

> *As when fire sets twigs ablaze and causes water to boil, come down to make Your name known to Your enemies and cause the nations to quake before You! For when You did awesome things that we did not expect, You came down, and the mountains trembled before You. Since ancient times no one has heard, no ear has perceived, no eye has seen any God besides You, who acts on behalf of those who wait for Him* (Isaiah 64:2-4).

EAST: God's glory—the sun rising. East wind brings judgment/hardship.

EATING: Feeding on something, e.g. Word of God or evil things. Meditation and gaining greater understanding.

East

ECHO: Word coming back. Word sphere against living revealed. Repercussions.

EGG, SEED: Delicate seed or promise. Sustenance. The possibility for growth—potential and development in any manner, revelation.

EGYPT: Bondage/slavery. Refuge—was refuge for Jesus. Old sin. Pre-Christian life.

Egypt

EIGHT: A new beginning. Circumcision of flesh.

EIGHTEEN: Bondage. God gave Israelites to Philistine for eighteen years.

He became angry with them. He sold them into the hands of the Philistines and the Ammonites, who that year shattered and crushed them. For eighteen years they oppressed all the Israelites on the east side of the Jordan in Gilead, the land of the Amorites (Judges 10:7-8).

And a woman was there who had been crippled by a spirit for eighteen years. She was bent over and could not straighten up at all. When Jesus saw her, He called her forward and said to her, "Woman, you are set free from your infirmity." Then He put His hands on her, and immediately she straightened up and praised God. Indignant because Jesus had healed on the Sabbath, the synagogue ruler said to the people, "There are six days for work. So come and be healed on those days, not on the Sabbath." The Lord answered him, "You hypocrites! Doesn't each of you on the Sabbath untie his ox or donkey from the stall and lead it out to give it water? Then should not this woman, a daughter of Abraham, whom satan has kept bound for eighteen long years, be set free on the Sabbath day from what bound her?" (Luke 13:11-16)

ELECTRICITY: Spiritual power of God; potential for God's flow.

Outlet for electricity: Possibility of being connected into the flow of the Holy Spirit.

Unplugged cord: Not connected to the power of the Spirit.

ELEMENTARY: The infant stage, not yet mature.

ELEVATOR: Moving up and down in levels of godly authority.

ELEVEN: Disorder, confusion, lawlessness.

Elevator

EMPLOYEE/SERVANTS: The one who is submitted to the authority. The actual person.

EMPLOYER/MASTER: Jesus. The authority, good or bad. Pastor. Evil leadership.

EXPLOSION: Quick outburst, generally positive. Sudden expansion or increase. Quick work or devastating change.

Explosion

EYES: Seer's anointing.

Winking: Concealed intention or cunning person.

Closed: Ignorance, spiritually blind, mostly self-imposed.

Eyes

FACE: Identity or characteristics. Image expression.

Face

FACTORY: Structured service in God's vineyard.

FALLING: Loss of support. Falling out of favor. Entering a time of trial/darkness/sin.

Factory

FAMILY: The Christian or spiritual family. Group of people in covenant or spirit of oneness; unified fellowship.

FAN: Stirring up of gifting. Something that brings relief or comfort. Make fire hotter. Increasing circulation.

FARMER: One who plants, nurtures, cares for new Christians. Pastor capable of sowing and reaping harvest. Jesus Christ.

Fan

FATHER: Father God, supplier of needs. Natural father of the bloodline. One who provides. The head of home or place.

FATHER-IN-LAW: Father figure within the organization. An advisor, spirit of delegation, head of another organization.

FEATHERS: Protective spiritual covering. Weightless. Something with which to move in the spiritual realm. Presence of God.

He will cover you with His feathers, and under His wings you will find refuge; His faithfulness will be your shield and rampart (Psalm 91:4).

Feathers

Say to them, "This is what the Sovereign Lord says: A great eagle with powerful wings, long feathers and full plumage of varied colors came to Lebanon. Taking hold of the top of a cedar, he broke off its topmost shoot and carried it away to a land of merchants, where he planted it in a city of traders. He took some of the seed of your land and put it in fertile soil. He planted it like a willow by abundant water, and it sprouted and became a low, spreading vine. Its branches turned toward him, but its roots remained under it. So it became a vine and produced branches and put out leafy boughs. But there was another great eagle with powerful wings and full plumage. The vine now sent out its roots toward him from the plot where it was planted and stretched out its branches to him for water" (Ezekiel 17:3-7).

FEEDING: To partake in a spiritual provision, good or evil.

FEET: A spiritual walk, heart attitude.

Barefoot: Humble before the presence of God.

Diseased: Spirit of offense.

Kicking: Not under authority or working against authority.

Lame: Crippled with unbelief, mind-set, negative stronghold.

Washing: Humble; duty of Christians.

Overgrown nails: Lack of care, not in proper order.

FENCE: Protection. Security. Self-imposed. Limitation. Stronghold.

Fence

How long will you assault a man? Would all of you throw him down—this leaning wall, this tottering fence? (Psalm 62:3)

Then the king of the North will come and build up siege ramps and will capture a fortified [fenced] city. The forces of the South will be powerless to resist; even their best troops will not have the strength to stand (Daniel 11:15).

FIELD: Life situation, things to do and accomplish. (Depends on the field and context.)

He gives rain on the earth, and sends waters on the fields (Job 5:10 NKJ).

FIFTEEN: Mercy, grace, liberty, rest, freedom.

FIFTY: Period or time of outpouring such as Pentecost. Number of Holy Spirit/jubilee/freedom/liberty.

FIGHT: To struggle with, to agonize, to war or resist something.

Contend, O Lord, with those who contend with me; fight against those who fight against me (Psalm 35:1).

Fight the good fight of the faith. Take hold of the eternal life to which you were called when you made your good confession in the presence of many witnesses (1 Timothy 6:12).

Remember those earlier days after you had received the light, when you stood your ground in a great contest [fight] *in the face of suffering* (Hebrews 10:32).

FINGER: Means of discernment. Spiritual sensitivity—feelings.

Pointed finger: Accusations, persecution, instructions, direction.

Finger of God: Work of God, authority of God.

Clenched: Pride.

Thumb: Apostle.

Index: Prophet.

Middle: Evangelist.

Small: Pastor.

FIRE: God's presence. Trial, persecution, burning fervency, emotion, longing, aching and craving. Power. Holy Spirit. Anger or judgment/punishment. Lake of fire, very different from tongue of fire.

Fire

Then the Lord rained down burning sulphur on Sodom and Gomorrah—from the Lord out of the heavens (Genesis 19:24).

FISH: New converts to the Lord. Newly recreated spirit of man. Miraculous provision of food.

"Come, follow Me," Jesus said, "and I will make you fishers of men" (Mark 1:17).

Fish

FIVE: Grace related to the fivefold ministry.

FLASH: Revelation or insight.

FLEA: Not plentiful. Inconvenience. Subtlety.

FLOOD: Judgment on those who use whatever power they have to inflict violence on others. Sin judged. Overcome. To be overcome and unable to recover.

From the west, men will fear the name of the Lord, and from the rising of the sun, they will revere His glory. For He will come like a pent-up flood that the breath of the Lord drives along (Isaiah 59:19).

I am going to bring floodwaters on the earth to destroy all life under the heavens, every creature that has the breath of life in it. Everything on earth will perish (Genesis 6:17).

FLOWERS: Man's glory of the flesh that is passing away. An offering. Glory of God. Beautiful expression of love. Renewal. Spring.

That fading flower, his glorious beauty, set on the head of a fertile valley, will be like a fig ripe before harvest—as soon as someone sees it and takes it in his hand, he swallows it (Isaiah 28:4).

Flower

But the one who is rich should take pride in his low position, because he will pass away like a wild flower (James 1:10).

For, "All men are like grass, and all their glory is like the flowers of the field; the grass withers and the flowers fall" (1 Peter 1:24).

Lily of the valley: Jesus.

Rose: Love, courtship, romance.

FLY: Evil spirits. Corruption. To possess by evil spirit. Results of unclean actions.

As dead flies give perfume a bad smell, so a little folly outweighs wisdom and honor (Ecclesiastes 10:1).

In that day the Lord will whistle for flies from the distant streams of Egypt and for bees from the land of Assyria (Isaiah 7:18).

FLYING: Highly powered by the Holy Spirit.

Who are these that fly along like clouds, like doves to their nests? (Isaiah 60:8)

Like birds hovering overhead, the Lord Almighty will shield Jerusalem; H will shield it and deliver it, H will "pass over" it and will rescue it (Isaiah 31:5).

He mounted the cherubim and flew; He soared on the wings of the wind (Psalm 18:10, 2 Samuel 22:11).

FOG: Not clear, uncertainty, concealed, vagueness. Wrath of God.

FOOD: Spiritual and physical nourishment, good or evil. To bring increase.

Food

They should collect all the food of these good years that are coming and store up the grain under the authority of Pharaoh, to be kept in the cities for food (Genesis 41:35).

FOREIGNER: A person outside the Christian faith (not a citizen of Heaven). Someone to be taught and cared for, and brought into the covenant.

FOREHEAD: Thought process and reasoning. Revelations. Retaining and recalling ability. Commitment to God.

FOREST: Growth in life (depending on the context). Place of danger and darkness where one can be easily lost and harmed. Confusion and lack of direction, uncultivated. A land covered with trees that are naturally planted is different from a park where man's hand is more evident.

Forest

The battle spread out over the whole countryside, and the forest claimed more lives that day than the sword (2 Samuel 18:8).

FORTY: Testing period, season of trial.

Moses was there with the Lord forty days and forty nights without eating bread or drinking water. And he wrote on the tablets the words of the covenant—the Ten Commandments (Exodus 34:28).

I brought you up out of Egypt, and I led you forty years in the desert to give you the land of the Amorites (Amos 2:10).

Where for forty days he was tempted by the devil. He ate nothing during those days, and at the end of them he was hungry (Luke 4:2).

FOUR: Worldly creation; four corners of the world; four seasons. Global implication or the four Gospels.

FOURTEEN: Double anointing. Recreation. Reproduction. Passover.

FOX: A cunning spirit. Craftiness, secretly or counter-productive.

Tobiah the Ammonite, who was at his side, said, "What they are building—if even a fox climbed up on it, he would break down their wall of stones!" (Nehemiah 4:3)

Catch for us the foxes, the little foxes that ruin the vineyards, our vineyards that are in bloom (Song of Solomon 2:15).

Your prophets, O Israel, are like jackals [foxes] *among ruins* (Ezekiel 13:4).

He replied, "Go tell that fox, 'I will drive out demons and heal people today and tomorrow, and on the third day I will reach My goal' " (Luke 13:32).

FREEZER: Storing spiritual food for future time.

FRIEND: Brother or sister in Christ. Yourself. Showing to have similar qualities. Faithful person.

FROG: Evil spirit. Makes a lot of noise, boastful. Sorcery. Lying nature. Issuing curses.

Frog

If you refuse to let them go, I will plague your whole country with frogs (Exodus 8:2).

He sent swarms of flies that devoured them, and frogs that devastated them (Psalm 78:45).

Then I saw three evil spirits that looked like frogs; they came out of the mouth of the dragon, out of the mouth of the beast and out of the mouth of the false prophet (Revelation 16:13).

FRONT SIDE: Looking ahead, something in the future.

FRUITS: Source of nourishment. Means of increase. Reward of labor. To bear something or child. Harvest. Come to fullness. Gifts of the Spirit. Fruit of our labor. Fruit of the womb. Fruit of the Holy Spirit, consisting of all the Christian virtues.

Fruits

FUEL: Source of energy. Source of food for the Spirit. Capable of reviving.

FURNACE: Source of heat, the heart, heated and painful experiences. Period of trial. Source of pruning. Center of holy activities.

Whoever does not fall down and worship will immediately be thrown into a blazing furnace (Daniel 3:6).

But as for you, the Lord took you and brought you out of the iron-smelting furnace, out of Egypt, to be the people of His inheritance, as you now are (Deuteronomy 4:20).

See, I have refined you, though not as silver; I have tested you in the furnace of affliction (Isaiah 48:10).

Gallows

GALLOWS: A place of severe punishment. A place of nemesis or a place of death.

So they hanged Haman on the gallows he had prepared for Mordecai. Then the king's fury subsided (Esther 7:10).

GAP: Breach. A weak spot. A loophole. An opening.

You have not gone up to the breaks in the wall to repair it for the house of Israel so that it will stand firm in the battle on the day of the Lord (Ezekiel 13:5).

I looked for a man among them who would build up the wall and stand before Me in the gap on behalf of the land so I would not have to destroy it, but I found none (Ezekiel 22:30).

GARAGE: Symbolic of storage. Potential or protection.

GARBAGE: Abandoned things. Corruption. Reprobate or unclean. Unclean spirit; departure from all that is godly. Something that is thrown away. Opinion of life without Jesus.

GARDEN: A piece of land that is cultivated, signifying the life situation as planned by God. Field of labor in life. A place of increase, fruitfulness and productivity. A place of rest or romance. Life of believer as a garden mastered by the Holy Spirit.

Now the Lord God had planted a garden in the east, in Eden; and there He put the man He had formed (Genesis 2:8).

The Lord will guide you always; He will satisfy your needs in a sunscorched land and will strengthen your frame. You will be like a wellwatered garden, like a spring whose waters never fail (Isaiah 58:11).

The woman said to the serpent, "We may eat fruit from the trees in the garden" (Genesis 3:2).

Then the man and his wife heard the sound of the Lord God as He was walking in the garden in the cool of the day, and they hid from the Lord God among the trees of the garden (Genesis 3:8).

GARDENING: An area of labor. A place of reward, increase, or harvest.

GARMENT: Covering.

Clean: Honor or mantle.

Dirty: The glory of God upon a person. Stained with sin.

GASOLINE: Source of energy. Faith filled/prayer. Danger. Sinful motives.

GATE: Doors, opening. Salvation. Entrance to something such as building, grounds, or cities. In biblical days, business bargaining negotiations were conducted at the gates. Passage into or out of a place.

Gate

All these cities were fortified with high walls and with gates and bars, and there were also a great many unwalled villages (Deuteronomy 3:5).

For He breaks down gates of bronze and cuts through bars of iron (Psalm 107:16).

I will go before you and will level the mountains; I will break down gates of bronze and cut through bars of iron (Isaiah 45:2).

The twelve gates were twelve pearls, each gate made of a single pearl. The great street of the city was of pure gold, like transparent glass (Revelation 21:21).

The Lord loves the gates of Zion more than all the dwellings of Jacob (Psalm 87:2).

GIANT: A powerful spiritual being e.g. an angel or demon. A challenging situation that needs to be overcome. Something that arouses fear.

We saw the Nephilim there (the descendants of Anak come from the Nephilim). We seemed like grasshoppers in our own eyes, and we looked the same to them (Numbers 13:33).

GIRDLE: To prepare for use; might potency. To strengthen for readiness. Gathering together of the strength within you.

GLOVES: Something that protects the means of service. Something that fits. Something that protects the means of productivity.

GOAT: Pertaining to foolishness. Carnal, fleshly. Not submitting to authority. Walking into sin. Need for repentance. Miscarriage of judgment, i.e. scapegoat.

Goat

GOLD: Of God. Seal of divinity. Honorable. God's glory. Faithful; endurance; holiness that endures. Symbol of honor; of high valor. Something valuable that endures.

I turned around to see the voice that was speaking to me. And when I turned I saw seven golden lampstands (Revelation 1:12).

Overlay it with pure gold, both inside and out, and make a gold molding around it (Exodus 25:11).

Make a table of acacia wood—two cubits long, a cubit wide and a cubit and a half high. Overlay it with pure gold and make a gold molding around it. Also make around it a rim a handbreadth wide and put a gold molding on the rim. Make four gold rings for the table and fasten them to the four corners, where the four legs are. The rings are to be close to the rim to hold the poles used in carrying the table. Make the poles of acacia wood, overlay them with gold and carry the table with them. And make its plates and dishes of pure gold, as well as its pitchers and bowls for the pouring out of offerings. Put the bread of the Presence on this table to be before Me at all times (Exodus 25:23-30).

In a large house there are articles not only of gold and silver, but also of wood and clay; some are for noble purposes and some for ignoble (2 Timothy 2:20).

GOVERNOR: The person who has the power in the place. Spiritual leader in the church, to a geographical region or evil principality. Authority; rulership; reigning.

GRANDCHILD: Blessing passed on from a previous generation. Spirit passed on from the past generation. Generation inheritance, good or bad. Heir. Spiritual offspring of your ministry.

GRANDMOTHER: Generational authority over the person. Spiritual inheritance. Past wisdom or gifting.

GRAPES: Fruit of the promised land. Successful agriculture or success in life. Pleasant to the eyes. Evidence of fertility.

Grapes

When I found Israel, it was like finding grapes in the desert; when I saw your fathers, it was like seeing the early fruit on the fig tree. But when they came to Baal Peor, they consecrated themselves to that shameful idol and became as vile as the thing they loved (Hosea 9:10).

"The days are coming," declares the Lord, "when the reaper will be overtaken by the plowman and the planter by the one treading grapes. New wine will drip from the mountains and flow from all the hills" (Amos 9:13).

Still another angel, who had charge of the fire, came from the altar and called in a loud voice to him who had the sharp sickle, "Take your sharp sickle and gather the clusters of grapes from the earth's vine, because its grapes are ripe" (Revelation 14:18).

When they reached the Valley of Eshcol, they cut off a branch bearing a single cluster of grapes. Two of them carried it on a pole between them, along with some pomegranates and figs (Numbers 13:23).

GRASS: Divinely provided; something meant to be maintained. Life. God's Word in seed form. Word of God.

Dried: Death of the flesh through repentance.

Mowed: Disciplined obedience.

GRASSHOPPER/LOCUST: A devastating situation. Instrument of God's judgment. Low self-esteem.

GRAVEYARD/GRAVE: Old tradition. Cultural reserve. Death. Demonic influence from the past. Buried potentials.

Let's swallow them alive, like the grave, and whole, like those who go down to the pit (Proverbs 1:12).

Grave

All your pomp has been brought down to the grave, along with the noise of your harps; maggots are spread out beneath you and worms cover you (Isaiah 14:11).

They came out of the tombs, and after Jesus' resurrection they went into the holy city and appeared to many people (Matthew 27:53).

GREY: Uncertainty, compromise, consisting of good and bad mixture.

GREEN: Life—can be good or evil life. Provision. Rest and peace.

GROOM: Christ. Marriage. Headship.

GUARD: Ability to keep on the right path. Spirit of protection/to be vigilant.

GUEST: Spiritual messenger. An angel or evil presence.

GUN: Instrument of demonic affliction. Spoken words that wound. Power of words in prayer. Dominion through speaking the Word of God.

Gun

HAIL: Means of judgment against God's enemies. Something that can cause considerable damage to crops, property, and life. Means of punishment for the wicked.

Therefore, at this time tomorrow I will send the worst hailstorm that has ever fallen on Egypt, from the day it was founded till now (Exodus 9:18).

When Moses stretched out his staff toward the sky, the Lord sent thunder and hail, and lightning flashed down to the ground. So the Lord rained hail on the land of Egypt; hail fell and lightning flashed back and forth. It was the worst storm in all the land of Egypt since it had become a nation (Exodus 9:23-24).

I will execute judgment upon him with plague and bloodshed; I will pour down torrents of rain, hailstones and burning sulfur on him and on his troops and on the many nations with him (Ezekiel 38:22).

HAMMER: Living Word. Preaching the Word hard and fast. Capable of breaking something to pieces. Something that smooths strong things such as metal or rocks. For building.

Hammer

The craftsman encourages the goldsmith, and he who smooths with the hammer spurs on him who strikes the anvil. He says of the welding, "It is good." He nails down the idol so it will not topple (Isaiah 41:7).

"Is not My word like fire," declares the Lord, "and like a hammer that breaks a rock in pieces?" (Jeremiah 23:29)

HANDS: Means of service. Means of expressing strength.

Clapping: Joy and worship.

Fist: Pride in one's strength; anger.

Covering face: Guilt or shame.

Holding hands: In agreement.

Left hand: Something spiritual.

Raised hands: Surrender or worshipping.

Right hand: Oath of allegiance. Means of power, of honor. Natural strengths.

Shaking hands: Coming to an agreement.

Stretched out hands: Surrender.

Trembling: To fear; spirit of fear; anxiety. Awe at God's presence.

Under thighs: In oaths.

Washing: Declaring innocence; to dissociate oneself.

HARLOT, PROSTITUTE: A tempting situation. Something that appeals to your flesh. Worldly desire. Pre-Christian habit that wants to resurrect. Enticement.

HARP: If used for God, praise and worship in Heaven and in the earth. Instrument for praise and worship. Could be used for idolatry.

HARVEST: Seasons of grace. Opportunities to share the gospel. Fruitfulness. Reward of labor and action.

Harp

HAT: Covering, protection, mantle, crown. Protection of the head.

HEAD: Lordship, authority. Jesus/God. Husband. Master/boss. Pastor. Mind, thoughts.

Hat

Anointed: Set apart for God's service.

Hands on head: Signifying sorrow.

HEDGE: God's safeguard, security, safety. Literally—loose stonewall without mortar. Protection. Supernatural or prophetic protection. God as hedge around His people. Where the very poor find shelter.

Why have you broken down its walls [hedge] *so that all who pass by pick its grapes?* (Psalm 80:12)

He then began to speak to them in parables: "A man planted a vineyard. He put a wall around it, dug a pit for the winepress and built a watchtower. Then he rented the vineyard to some farmers and went away on a journey (Mark 12:1).

HEEL: The crushing power.

HELICOPTER: Spirit-powered for spiritual warfare. One-man ministry.

HELMET: The awareness and inner assurance of salvation. God's promise.

Helicopter

HIGH SCHOOL: Moving into a higher level of walk with God. Capable of giving the same to others.

HIGHWAY: Holy way; the path of life. Truth of God, Christ. Predetermined path of life, or path of life that enjoys high volume usage. May lead to good or evil destinations.

Dead end: A course of action that will lead to nothing.

Gravel: Way; God's Word; stony ground.

Muddy: Difficult path; not clear; uncertain path.

Construction: In preparation, change.

HILLS: A place of exaltation. Uplift high above the natural. Throne of God. Mount Zion.

HIPS: Reproduction. Relating to reproduction or supporting structure.

HONEY: Sweet; strength; wisdom. Spirit of God. The abiding anointing. The sweet Word of our Lord. Standard of measure for pleasant things. The best product of the land. Abundance. A land flowing with milk and honey. Food in times of scarcity.

> *Then their father Israel said to them, "If it must be, then do this: Put some of the best products of the land in your bags and take them down to the man as a gift—a little balm and a little honey, some spices and myrrh, some pistachio nuts and almonds* (Genesis 43:11).

> *He will not enjoy the streams, the rivers flowing with honey and cream* (Job 20:17).

> *So I have come down to rescue them from the hand of the Egyptians and to bring them up out of that land into a good and spacious land, a land flowing with milk and honey—the home of the Canaanites, Hittites, Amorites, Perizzites, Hivites and Jebusites* (Exodus 3:8).

> *Honey and curds, sheep, and cheese from cows' milk for David and his people to eat. For they said, "The people have become hungry and tired and thirsty in the desert"* (2 Samuel 17:29).

HORNS: The source of anointed power. The power of the kings.

HORSE: Of great strength; powerful in warfare. Spirit of tenaciousness, not double-minded. A ministry that is powerful and capable of competing. Strength under control, such as meekness. God's judgment.

Horse that kicks: Threatening, or opposition to the agreed terms.

Black: Lack.

Bay (flame-colored): Power, fire.

Pale: Spirit of death.

Red: Danger; passion; blood of Jesus.

White: Purity or righteousness.

Blue: Spiritual.

Brown: Repented, born-again.

Green: Life, mortal.

Grey: In between black and white. Vague, hazy.

Orange: Danger, evil.

Pink: Flesh. Relating to desire and decision based on the mind.

Purple: Something related to royalty. Noble in character. Riches.

Yellow: Gift from God or cowardliness, fear.

HOSPITAL: A gift of healing/anointing or caring or love. Edifying others.

HOTEL: A place of gathering, a temporary place of meeting. A transit place of meeting, church; a transit situation.

HOUSE: One's spiritual and emotion house. Personality. Church.

House

HUSBAND: Jesus Christ. Actual person.

HUSBAND, EX-HUSBAND: Previous head over you—something that had control over you in the past.

INCENSE: Prayer, worship, praise. Acceptable unto God.

IRON: Something of strength, powerful. Strict rules/powerful strongholds.

IRONING: The process of correction by instructions, teaching. To talk things over. Working out problem relationships. Turning from sin.

ISLAND: Something related to the island. What the island is known for, or its name.

ISRAEL: The nation of Israel. The Christian community; the redeemed ones. Authority that comes from God over men. People of God.

JERUSALEM: The establishment of peace. Chosen place by God. The city of God.

JEWELRY: Valuable possessions. God's people. Gifted person who has received abilities from the Lord. Something or someone valued by the dreamer.

Jewelry

JUDGE: Father God. Authority. Anointed to make decisions. Jesus Christ. Unjust ruler.

KANGAROO: Something that is not based on the truth. Prejudiced. Rushing to conclusion.

Judge

KEY: The authority to something, claim to ownership. Prophetic authority. Kingdom authority.

KISS: Coming to agreement, covenant. Seductive process. Enticement. Deception or betrayal. Betrayal from a trusted friend or brother/sister in Christ.

KITCHEN: A place of preparing spiritual food. Hunger for the word of God.

KNEELING: Surrender; praying; art of submission.

KNEES: Reverence; prayerfulness; submission.

KNIVES, SWORD: Word of God. Speaking against some-one.

Knife

LADDER: A means of change in spiritual position. Means of escape from captivity.

LAMB/SHEEP: Jesus. Believer. Gentleness. Blamelessness.

LAME: Shortcomings. A flaw in one's walk with God. Limitation.

LAMP: Source of light. Inward part of man or spirit. Holy Spirit.

LAND: Inheritance. Promise given by God.

Lamp

Newly cleared land: Newly revealed area of God's promise.

Ripe on the land: Fruitful work of the ministry.

Bare earth or dust: Curse, bareness.

Neglected, unwanted land: Neglected promise or inheritance.

LAUGH: Rejoicing. Joy or sarcasm.

LAUGHING: Outburst of excitement or joy.

LAVA: Enemy.

LAWYER: Jesus Christ. The accuser of brethren. Pertaining to legalism. Mediator.

LEAD (METAL): Heavy burden; heavy thing.

LEAVEN: Sin that spreads to others. False belief system.

LEAVES: Trees with healthy leaves are planted by the rivers of life; healing of the nation.

Dry leaves: Pressures of life.

Leaf

LEFT: That which is of the Spirit. That which is not natural with man. God manifested through the flesh of man.

Who has gone into heaven and is at God's right hand—with angels, authorities and powers in submission to Him (1 Peter 3:22).

LEGS: Means of support. Spiritual strength to walk in life.

Legs, female: Power to entice.

LEOPARD: Powerful, either good or bad. Permanent. Unchanging character.

LEMON: Something gone sour; bitter doctrine.

LEVIATHAN: Ancestral spirit of demonic nature; difficult to eliminate—only God can deal with it.

Lemon

LIBRARY: A place of knowledge. Schooling. Wisdom.

LICE: Concerted attempt to smear you. Accusation, shame.

Library

LIFTING HANDS: Total surrender. Giving worship to God.

LIGHT: Illumination on the established truth. No longer hidden; to show forth.

Dim light: Showing the need for the fullness of the knowledge of the Word.

Absence of light: Lack of understanding; absence of God.

Small lamp or flashlight: Walking in partial founding of the Word.

LIGHTNING: God's voice; the Lord interrupting an activity to get man's attention. Something happening very quickly.

LIMOUSINE: Call of God. Pride or exhibitionism.

Lightning

LION: Conquering nature of Jesus (majority of the time). A powerful spirit, good or bad.

LIPS: Word of God. Enticement. Means of testifying. Offering. Speak falsehood/accusation.

LIVING ROOM: Part of your personality that is opened to others to see.

LOST IN WHAT IN THE NATURAL IS A FAMILIAL ENVIRONMENT (DIRECTION): Indicating inner confusions or indecision in the dreamer.

MACHINES: Power and mechanism of the Spirit.

MAGGOT: Filthiness or the lust of the flesh. Corruption.

MAN (UNKNOWN): A spiritual messenger, either God' messenger or evil. Jesus.

MANNA: God's miraculous provision. Coming directly from God. Glory of God. Bread of life.

MAP: Word of God. Instruction. Direction.

MARBLE: Beauty. Majesty of God.

Map

MARK: Something that distinguishes. Symbol. To set apart. Mark of God or devil.

MARRIAGE: Going deeper into things of God (intimacy). A covenant process. Actual marriage. Jesus Christ's union with the Church.

MEAT: Something meant for the spiritually mature. Strong doctrine.

> *I gave you milk, not solid food, for you were not yet ready for it. Indeed, you are still not ready* (1 Corinthians 3:2).

Meat

> *But strong meat belongeth to them that are of full age, even those who by reason of use have their senses exercised to discern both good and evil* (Hebrews 5:14 KJV).

MERCY SEAT: Indicating the mercy of God. Kingship of the Lord. The throne of God. God's love.

MICE: Something that eats up valuables secretly. Devourer. Spirit of timidity or fear. Evil that can multiple rapidly.

MICROPHONE: Amplification of the Word of God. Preaching. The prophetic ministry. Ability to influence many people.

Microphone

MICROSCOPE: Need to look more carefully. Obtaining clearer vision. To magnify something, whether good or bad.

MICROWAVE OVEN: May indicate lack of patience. Looking for easy option. Quick acting process.

Microscope

MIDDLE/JUNIOR HIGH: Medium level equipping by God.

MILK: Good nourishment. Elementary teaching.

MIRROR: Something that enables you to look more closely. Reflecting on something. Word of God revealing the need for change. Self-consciousness; vanity.

MISCARRIAGE: To lose something at the preparatory stage, whether good or bad. Plans aborted.

MONEY: God's favor. Spiritual and natural wealth. Spiritual authority, power. Man's strength. Greed.

MOON: Indicating the rulership. To reign in the night seasons. Light of God at dark season of life.

Money

> *God made two great lights—the greater light to govern the day and the lesser light to govern the night. He also made the stars* (Genesis 1:16).

MOON TO BLOOD: The Church being prosecuted. Something bright in darkness.

MORNING: The beginning of something. Light of God after dark season of life. Sins being revealed. Rejoicing.

MOTH: Insect that dwells in dark places. Causes loss by deceitfulness. Corruption and deterioration.

MOTHER: The Church. Jerusalem. Actual person. Spiritual mother. Carer/teacher.

Moth

MOTHER-IN-LAW: A church that is not your actual church. Actual person. False teacher.

MOTOR, ENGINE AND BATTERY: The source of power and of the anointing.

MOTORCYCLE: Spirit-powered personal ministry. Loner. Show-off pride or exhibitionism.

MOUNTAIN: Great power and strength, whether good or bad. A place of revelation or meeting with God or God's glory. Obstacle, difficulty.

MOUTH: Instrument of witnessing, good or bad. Speaking evil or good words. Something from which come the issues of life. Words coming against you.

MOVING: Change in spiritual and emotional well-being. Changing situation; a change is imminent.

MOVING VAN: A time or period of change, either in the natural or in the spirit.

MUSIC: Praise and worship, good or bad. Flowing in spiritual gift. Teaching. Admonishing. A message.

MUSTARD SEED: Faith. Value or power of faith. Sowing is faith; Word of God. God's promise.

> *He replied, "Because you have so little faith. I tell you the truth, if you have faith as small as a mustard seed, you can say to this mountain, 'Move from here to there' and it will move. Nothing will be impossible for you"* (Matthew 17:20).

NAILS: Makes something more permanent. The way Jesus dealt with our sins.

NAME: The identity of something; designate; rank or status. Meaning of the name.

NATION: Could represent the characteristics of the nation. The calling related to the nation. The actual nation.

> *America*: Cowboy.
>
> *France*: Romance.
>
> *Germany*: Hardworking. World war.
>
> *Jews*: Business minded.

NECK: Stubborn, strong willed.

> *Stiff-necked*: Rebellious.

NEST: Security that is not real; God's place of rest.

NET: To trap, ensnare. The plans of the enemy. To win souls.

. *Nest*

NEW: New condition.

NEWSPAPER: Proclamation. Bringing something to the public. Prophetic utterance.

NIGHT: Time of trial or difficulty. Lack of God's lights or understanding. Without involvement of the Spirit.

NINE: Fruit of the Spirit or gift of the Spirit; harvest.

NINETEEN: Faith, repentance.

NOISE: Irritation that is intrusive. Sound that draws attention.

NORTH: Refers to great powers that will come.

NOSE: Discerning spirit. Intruding into people's privacy. Discernment, good or bad. Gossiper.

NOSEBLEED: Strife. Need to strengthen your discerning.

Nose

OCEAN: Masses of people.

OIL: The anointing. Prosperity. Holy Spirit. Grace/mercy of God. Medicine. Joy.

OLD: Old ways.

OLD MAN: Pre-Christian self. Spirit of wisdom.

ONE: New beginning. Unity (divinity). Deity.

ONE HUNDRED: Fullness. One hundred-fold reward. The promise.

Isaac planted crops in that land and the same year reaped a hundred-fold, because the Lord blessed him (Genesis 26:12).

ONE HUNDRED FIFTY: The promise and the Holy Spirit.

ONE HUNDRED TWENTY: The beginning of the work of Holy Spirit.

In those days Peter stood up among the believers (a group numbering about a hundred and twenty) (Acts 1:15).

ORANGE: Warning, danger ahead, caution needed.

OVEN: The heart of the matter. Of high intensity. Fervency.

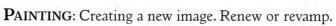

Oven

OVERSLEPT: There is a chance of missing a divine appointment.

PAINTING: Creating a new image. Renew or revamp.

PARACHUTING: Bail out, escape and flee.

PARK: A place of rest, worship, tranquillity. A temporary place. A place of peace. A place of romance. A place of meditation, exercise, and leisure.

Parachuting

PARROT: Something that mimics. Not the original.

PATH: The path of life. Personal walk with God. Directions in life.

PEACOCK: Something of pride. Generally adornment of royal courts.

PEARL: Something of value. Established truth of God. Glory of Heaven.

PEN/PENCIL: Pertaining to writing. Words that are written. To make permanent.

PERFUME: Aroma of something. The glory of God. Fragrance of Holy Spirit or anointing.

Perfume

PICTURE: Something relating to images. To keep in memory. To honor.

   Frames: Mind-set; mentality.

   Golden frames: Divine seal.

   Old frame: Outdated.

PIG: Unclean spirit. Spirit of religion. Caged by mind-set. Phoney, not trustworthy. Selfish, hypocritical.

PILLAR: The main support of something. Spiritual and natural. Foundational truths.

Pillar

PINK: Flesh or natural desire. Not showing great passion for the things of God.

PIT: Enticement, trap; a hole on the pathway.

PLATTER: Something on which to present things.

PLAY: Life competition. Spiritual warfare/contention.

PLAYING: Reflective of true-life situation. The game of life.

PLOW: Preparing the heart to receive the Word of God. Cracking fallow grounds hardened by sin.

POISON: Evil and deadly teaching or doctrine.

POLICE: Spiritual authority. Having power to enforce purpose, whether good or bad. Pastor, elders. Angels or demons. Enforcer of a curse or of the law.

PORCH: Public part of the building, exhibition. Easily seen and openly displayed.

POSTAGE STAMP: The seal of authority. Authorization. Empowered.

POST-MORTEM: Examination of what has happened. Giving testimony.

POT: The vessel or container, e.g. tradition. A person.

PREGNANCY: In the process of reproducing; preparatory stage. The promise of God. The Word of God as seed. Prophetic word.

PREGNANCY, LABOR PAINS: Process of birthing something, whether good or bad. Final stages of trial or preparation; wilderness period.

PREACHER/PASTOR (PRIEST AND PROPHET): A person who represents God. Timely message from God. Spiritual authority.

PRISON: A place where a person is restricted and where human rights are limited. A place of bondage or confinement. Often indicates a place of depression; areas of stronghold bondage.

PRISONER: The lost soul.

PURPLE: Related to royalty. Kingly anointing or authority.

> *One of those listening was a woman named Lydia, a dealer in purple cloth from the city of Thyatira, who was a worshiper of God. The Lord opened her heart to respond to Paul's message* (Acts 16:14).

PURSE/WALLET: Treasure, heart, personal identity; precious and valuable.

Empty: Bankrupt.

RABBIT: Evil spirit. Something capable of carnal multiplication.

RADIO: Continuous broadcasting of news, nuisance. Prophetic utterance. Teaching gospel.

Radio

RAFT: Without purpose or direction.

RAGS: Poverty; humility or lack.

RAILROAD TRACK: Tradition; unchanging habit. Stubborn. Caution, danger.

RAIN: Blessings, God's Word. Outpouring of the Spirit. Hindrance, trial or disappointment.

> **Drought**: Lack of blessing. Absence of the presence of God.

RAINBOW: Sign of God's covenant. Sign of natural agreement.

RAINING: The blessing from God. Testing time or trial.

RAM: Satanic occult.

RAT: Rubbish (sin), left out to eat. A passion that is unclean or something that feeds it.

REAP: Harvest. Reward of effort, good or bad.

REAPING: Reward of labor.

RED: Passion. Blood of Jesus. Strong feeling, danger, anger. Heated emotion and bloody. Jesus. Zeal, enthusiasm.

REED: Weakness: spiritual or natural. Too weak to be relied on.

REFRIGERATOR: Where "issues" are kept. Heart issues. Motivation. Thoughts. Storing up spiritual food for the right time.

> **Stored food**: Things stored in the heart.
>
> **Spoiled food**: To harbor a grudge, unclean thoughts, or desires.

Refrigerator

REFUGE: The place of protection, safety, or security.

REINS: A means of control or to restrain.

RENDING: Sorrow or disagreement. To tear apart as sign of anger. Grief, repentance, sorrow, disagreement.

REST: A state of stillness or inactivity, tranquility. A place where you can receive from God. Laziness.

RESTAURANT: A place of choice regarding the spiritual food you need. A place where the fivefold ministry is taught.

RESTING: Not in activity; lax.

RIGHT: Natural inclination, authority, or power. What you are naturally able to do.

RIGHT TURN: Natural change.

RING: Never-ending, unchanging, uninterrupted. Unity of purpose in a place. Covenant relationship. Relating to God's authority.

Wedding ring: Symbol of our covenant with God. Marriage between man and woman.

Engagement ring: Promise. Sign of commitment.

Ring worn as jewelry: Vanity, worldliness.

RIVER: Movement of God. Flow of the Spirit. River as an obstacle. Trial.

Deep: Deep things of God.

Muddy: Operating in mixtures, flesh and spirit.

Dangerous currents: Difficulty in moving in the flow of the Spirit. Danger ahead.

Dried up: Lack of the presence of God; traditions or legalism. Empty of spiritual power.

ROACHES: Unclean. Something that can cause and thrive on sin.

ROBE: The true covering from God. Righteousness; right standing with God.

ROCK: Jesus Christ; solid foundation. Obstacle. A place of refuge. Stumbling block.

And drank the same spiritual drink; for they drank from the spiritual rock that accompanied them, and that rock was Christ (1 Corinthians 10:4).

He is the Rock, His works are perfect, and all His ways are just. A faithful God who does no wrong, upright and just is He (Deuteronomy 32:4).

ROCKET: A ministry or person with great power or potential for deep things of the Spirit. Capable of quick take-off and great speed.

Rocket

ROCKING: Reflective.

ROCKING CHAIR: Long standing in nature, intercession, recollection, prayer, relaxation, old age.

ROD: Staff or scepter of authority. To guard. Discipline.

The rod of correction imparts wisdom, but a child left to himself disgraces his mother (Proverbs 29:15).

Even though I walk through the valley of the shadow of death, I will fear no evil, for You are with me; Your rod and Your staff, they comfort me (Psalm 23:4).

ROLLER COASTER: Something that moves up and down. Swings of season or moods. Faith needing more faith.

ROLLER SKATES: Skillful walk with God. Speedy progress. Fast but may be dangerous.

ROOF: Zone of mind, thinking, meditation. Spiritual rather than the natural. Revelations from above; covering.

ROOT: The origin of something. The source of something. The heart of the matter, good or bad. The motives.

A shoot will come up from the stump of Jesse; from his roots a Branch will bear fruit (Isaiah 11:1).

In the morning, as they went along, they saw the fig tree withered from the roots (Mark 11:20).

ROPE/CORD: Something used in binding either. In covenant or in bondage.

ROUND (SHAPE): Never-ending. Favor, love, or mercy.

ROWBOAT: A ministry that intervenes for others. Offering earnest prayers.

ROWING: Working at something, to labor in spirit. Travailing in the spirit. Hard work.

RUG: To cover up something. Protection.

RUNNING: Trying to catch up with something. Hard work. Race.

SACRIFICE: To give up something. To lay down one's life for another. Something to cover up or wash away.

But King David replied to Araunah, "No, I insist on paying the full price. I will not take for the Lord what is yours, or sacrifice a burnt offering that costs me nothing" (1 Chronicles 21:24).

SALT: Something that adds value. Something that preserves. Something that purifies. To make to last.

You are the salt of the earth. But if the salt loses its saltiness, how can it be made salty again? It is no longer good for anything, except to be thrown out and trampled by men (Matthew 5:13).

Let your conversation be always full of grace, seasoned with salt, so that you may know how to answer everyone (Colossians 4:6).

SALT WATER: To add flavor. To cleanse.

SANCTUARY: A sacred place. A place set apart for spiritual offering, sacrifices. A place of immunity or rest. An asylum, a refuge.

Observe my Sabbaths and have reverence for my sanctuary. I am the Lord (Leviticus 26:2).

On the contrary, it is to be a witness between us and you and the generations that follow, that we will worship the Lord at His sanctuary with our burnt offerings, sacrifices and fellowship offerings. Then in the future your descendants will not be able to say to ours, "You have no share in the Lord" (Joshua 22:27).

SAND: Symbolic of work of flesh. Not suitable for foundation. Numerous. Seeds. Promises.

But You have said, "I will surely make you prosper and will make your descendants like the sand of the sea, which cannot be counted" (Genesis 32:12).

But everyone who hears these words of mine and does not put them into practice is like a foolish man who built his house on sand (Matthew 7:26).

SCEPTER: Staff of authority. Office. Staff of sovereignty.

The scepter will not depart from Judah, nor the ruler's staff from between his feet, until He comes to whom it belongs and the obedience of the nations is His (Genesis 49:10).

Scepter

Your throne, O God, will last for ever and ever; a scepter of justice will be the scepter of your kingdom (Psalm 45:6).

SCHOOL, CLASSROOM: Training period, a place of teaching. A ministry with teaching anointing.

SCORPION: Highly demonic spirit or any evil spirit. Something that could be poisonous.

SEA: Great multitude of people. Nations of the world. Unsettled, as the mark of a sea. Something by which to reach the nations. Great obstacle.

Four great beasts, each different from the others, came up out of the sea (Daniel 7:3).

SEACOAST: Transition phase. Borderland.

SEAL: Confirmation or authenticity or guarantee. Mark of God's approval or belonging. Mark of evil.

SEA OF GLASS: Peaceful and clear. Symbol of revelation. Stillness/transparency.

SEAT: The power base. Rulership. Authority. Coming to rest. A place of mercy.

SEED: Word of God. Promise. Something capable of giving rise to many or greater things, whether good or bad.

SERPENT: Symbol of satan. Kingdom of the world. An accursed thing or cunning.

Sna   *ng on a pole, stick, tree)*: Emblem of Christ on the
cros

Vip   o or persecution.

Pyt   it of divination.

Ra   words against the dreamer.

Fa   :rous intentions coming against the dreamer.

Co   s, capable of forming hooded neck, and can send off
po   a distance. Evil words that can spread far.

An   :ills by squeezing out air (spiritual life) from the
victim.

SEVEN: The number of perfection, completion, or finished work. Rest. A time of blessing or holy time. Freedom.

Remember the Sabbath day by keeping it holy. Six days you shall labor and do all your work, but the seventh day is a Sabbath to the Lord your God. On it you shall not do any work, neither you, nor your son or daughter, nor your manservant or maidservant, nor your animals, nor the alien within your gates. For in six days the Lord made the heavens and the earth, the sea, and all that is in them, but He rested on the seventh day. Therefore the Lord blessed the Sabbath day and made it holy (Exodus 20:8-11).

These are the laws you are to set before them: If you buy a Hebrew servant, he is to serve you for six years. But in the seventh year, he shall go free, without paying anything (Exodus 21:1-2).

SEVENTEEN: Spiritual process of maturation. Not yet matured.

This is the account of Jacob. Joseph, a young man of seventeen, was tending the flocks with his brothers, the sons of Bilhah and the sons of Zilpah, his father's wives, and he brought their father a bad report about them (Genesis 37:2).

SEVENTY: Impartation of God's Spirit /increase/restoration.

The Lord said to Moses: "Bring me seventy of Israel's elders who are known to you as leaders and officials among the people. Have them come to the Tent of Meeting, that they may stand there with you. I will come down and speak with you there, and I will take of the Spirit that is on you and put the Spirit on them. They will help you carry the burden of the people so that you will not have to carry it alone (Numbers 11:16-17).

SEVENTY-FIVE: Period for purification and separation. Abraham was 75 when he set out from Haran.

So Abram left, as the Lord had told him; and Lot went with him. Abram was seventy-five years old when he set out from Haran (Genesis 12:4).

SEWAGE: Something that carries away waste. Good appearance but carrying waste within. Waste that could defile flesh.

SEWING: Putting together something. Amendment; union; counselling.

SEXUAL ENCOUNTER: Soulish desires.

Sexual encounter with old lover: You desire your old life.

SHADOW: Reflection of something. The spiritual cover. A place of safety, security. Only partially illuminated. Poor resemblance of. Delusion or imitation. Imperfect or lacking the real substance.

He who dwells in the shelter of the Most High will rest in the shadow of the Almighty (Psalm 91:1).

Dark shadows: Demons.

SHEPHERD: Jesus Christ, God. Leader, good or bad. Ability to separate goat from sheep. Selfless person.

Then he blessed Joseph and said, "May the God before whom my fathers Abraham and Isaac walked, the God who has been my shepherd all my life to this day" (Genesis 48:15).

I am the good shepherd. The good shepherd lays down his life for the sheep (John 10:11).

Wherever I have moved with all the Israelites, did I ever say to any of their rulers whom I commanded to shepherd My people Israel, "Why have you not built Me a house of cedar?" (2 Samuel 7:7)

SHIELD: A protective thing. God's truth. Faith in God.

After this, the word of the Lord came to Abram in a vision: "Do not be afraid, Abram. I am your shield, your very great reward" (Genesis 15:1).

Shield

In addition to all this, take up the shield of faith, with which you can extinguish all the flaming arrows of the evil one (Ephesians 6:16).

The Lord is my strength and my shield; my heart trusts in Him, and I am helped. My heart leaps for joy and I will give thanks to Him in song (Psalm 28:7).

SHIP: A big ministry capable of influencing large numbers of people.

Battleship: Built for effective spiritual warfare.

Crashing: End of the ministry or end of one phase.

Fast: Operating in great power.

Large: Large area of influence.

Sinking: Out of line with the purpose of God, losing spiritual control.

Small: Small or personal.

On dry ground: Without the move of the Spirit. Moving more with the work of the flesh. (A miracle, if moving on dry ground.)

SHOES: Readiness to spread the gospel. Knowledge of the Word of God.

And with your feet fitted with the readiness that comes from the gospel of peace (Ephesians 6:15).

Shoes

Boots: Equipped for spiritual warfare.

Does not fit: Walking in something you're not called to.

Giving away: Depending on the context, equipping others.

High heels: Seduction/discomfort.

Need of shoes: Not dwelling on the Word of God. In need of comfort or protection.

New shoes: Getting new understanding of the gospel. Fresh mandate from God.

Putting on: Preparation for a spiritual journey.

Slippers: Too comfortable or too lax.

Snowshoes: Faith, walking in the Spirit, supported by faith in the Word of God.

Taking off: Honoring God, ministering to the Lord.

Taking someone else's shoes off: To show respect.

Tennis shoes: Spiritual giftedness. Running the race of life.

SHOPPING CENTER, MARKETPLACE: Ministry that has multifaceted giftedness within its midst. Coming to a place of choices that may lead to not being single-minded. Could also indicate the various methods of the enemy strategies.

SHOULDER: The responsibility; the authority.

Broad shoulders: Capable of handling much responsibility.

Bare female shoulders: Enticement.

Drooped shoulders: Defeated attitude. Overworked; over tired. Burned-out.

SHOVEL: Digging up something. To smear someone.

SICKLE: Reaping. Word of God. The harvest.

Shovel

SIEVE: To separate the impure from the pure. Trial or testing.

> *For I will give the command, and I will shake the house of Israel among all the nations as grain is shaken in a sieve, and not a pebble will reach the ground* (Amos 9:9).

Sickle

SIFT: Separation by testing.

> *Simon, Simon, Satan has asked to sift you as wheat* (Luke 22:31).

SIGN: A witness of something. A foreshadow. To draw attention to something.

Crossroad/intersection: A place for decision. Time for change.

Stop sign: Stop and pray for guidance.

Yield: A sign of submission.

SIGNATURE: Commitment and ownership or take responsibility for.

SILVER: Symbol of redemption. Understanding, knowledge. Something of valor, worldly knowledge, betrayal. Furnace of affliction.

SINGING: The words of the song = message from God. Rejoicing. Heart overflow.

SISTER: Sister in Jesus Christ. Actual person. Similar qualities in you.

SISTER-IN-LAW: Same as sister. A Christian in another fellowship. A relationship without much depth. Actual person. Person with similar qualities.

SITTING: A place of authority, position in power. Throne of God or seat of satan.

SIX: The number of man. Symbol of satan. Pride in the work of man.

SIX-SIX-SIX: Number of satan. Mark of the beast. Number of human hubris.

> *This calls for wisdom. If anyone has insight, let him calculate the number of the beast, for it is man's number. His number is 666* (Revelation 13:18).

SIXTEEN: Set free by love. The power of love or salvation. Sixteen characteristics of love mentioned in First Corinthians 13.

SKIING: Stepping out in faith. The power of faith. Smooth riding in God is provision. Making rapid process.

SKINS: The covering of.

SKY: Above the natural. God's presence. Related to God or high things of the Spirit.

SKYSCRAPER: A ministry or person who has a built-up structure to function on multilevels. A church or person with prophetic giftedness. High level of spiritual experience. Revelation.

Skyscraper

SLEEPING: Being overtaken. Not being conscious of something. Hidden. Laziness. State of rest; danger. Out of control.

> *Overslept*: In danger of missing a divine appointment.

SMILE: Sign of friendliness. Act of kindness. To agree with.

SMILING: Sign of friendship. Seductive process.

SMOKE: The manifested glory of God. Prayers of saints. Praise; worship. Sign of something. Hindrance.

SNAKE: Backbiting; divination; false accusations; false prophecies. Gossip; long tales; slander.

Snake

SNARE: A trap. The fear of man. Bring into bondage.

SNOW: Favor of God. Totally pure.

> *He spreads the snow like wool and scatters the frost like ashes* (Psalm 147:16).

> *As the rain and the snow come down from heaven, and do not return to it without watering the earth and making it bud and flourish, so that it yields seed for the sower and bread for the eater* (Isaiah 55:10).

> *As I looked, thrones were set in place, and the Ancient of Days took His seat. His clothing was as white as snow; the hair of His head was white like wool. His throne was flaming with fire, and its wheels were all ablaze* (Daniel 7:9).

> *Dirty snow*: No longer pure.

SOAP: Something that cleans. Forgiveness. Interceding for others.

SOCKS: Reflective of the state of the heart as the fertile ground for the Word of God. Peace. Protection of the feet.

> *White socks*: Heart and walk before God that is unblemished.

> *Dirty or torn socks:* Heart and walk before God that is blemished.

SOLDIER: Spiritual warfare. Call for more prayers, fasting, worship. A period of trial or persecution.

SON: A ministry or gifting from God. Actual child who has similar traits to you. Child of God.

SOUR: Corrupted. False.

SOUTH: A place of peace. Source of refreshment. The natural inclination.

SOWING: Planning for the future, good or bad. Spreading the Word of God.

SPEAKING: Revealing the contents of your heart. Proclamation.

SPEAR: Words, whether good or bad. Word of God. Evil words, curses.

SPIDER: An evil spirit that works by entrapping people. False doctrine.

Spider

SPOT: A fault. Contamination.

  Without spot: Glorious Church.

SPRINKLING: Spiritual change by washing away dirt. Cleansing, purifying, consecrating.

SQUARE: Tradition. Mind-set. Worldly and blind to the truth.

STADIUM: Tremendous impact.

STAFF: Symbol of authority. Part of authority.

STAIRS: Means of bringing about changes.

  Down: Demotion; backslide; failure.

  Guardrail: Safety; precaution; warning to be careful.

Staff

STANDING: Firmness in faith. Committed to the belief. Not finished.

  Straight: No crookedness but in the correct direction.

STARS: Important personality. Great number. Descendant. Supernatural. Jesus Christ.

  Falling star: Apostate Church.

STONE: Jesus Christ—chief cornerstone. Hard and sturdy foundation. Word of God. Defiance.

STONING SOMEONE: Involved in malicious accusation of others. Unforgiveness. Act of wickedness.

  Dragged him out of the city and began to stone him. Meanwhile, the witnesses laid their clothes at the feet of a young man named Saul (Acts 7:58).

STORM: Trial. Testing period. Satanic attacks.

  Before very long, a wind of hurricane force, called the "northeaster," swept down from the island. The ship was caught by the storm and could not head into the wind; so we gave way to it and were driven along (Acts 27:14-15).

  White storm: God's power, revival.

STRAIGHT: To be fixed in attitude. Going in the right direction.

STUMBLING: To make mistakes, to fail, in error. Lack of the truth.

SUICIDE: Act of self-destruction, foolishness. Sinful behavior. Pride. Lack of hope.

SUITCASE: On the move. Transition. Private walk with God.

Suitcase

SUMMER: Time of harvest. The opportune time. Fruits of the Spirit.

SUN: The light of God. The truth. Glory of God.

SUPPER: The body and blood of Jesus. Marriage supper. God's provision. God's enabling power.

SWEATING: Signs of intense work of the flesh. Much work without Holy Spirit. Difficult and agonizing time.

SWEEPING: Getting rid of sinful things. Cleaning the place from evil. The process of making clean. Repentance. Correcting process.

SWEET: Something gratifying. Reflection in the Word of God. Communion with the Spirit.

SWIMMING: Moving in spiritual gifts. Prophetic utterance.

SWIMMING POOL: Church, place or provision available for moving in the Spirit.

> *Dirty or dry*: Corrupt or apostate.

SWING: Moving in ups and downs of life.

SWINGING: Full flow of peace.

> *High*: Overindulgence. Taking unnecessary risks.

SWORD: Word of God. Evil words.

Sword

TABLE: A place of agreement or covenant. To iron issues out. Altar. Community, fellowship.

> *You prepare a table before me in the presence of my enemies. You anoint my head with oil; my cup overflows* (Psalm 23:5).

TAIL: The end of something. The least of something. The last time.

TAR: Covering; bitterness.

TARES: Children of darkness. Evil ones. Degenerates. Deceptive, e.g. grains.

TASTING: To experience something good or bad. Judging something. Try something out.

TEA: A place or time of rest. Revelation or grace of God. Soothing.

TEACHER: Jesus Christ. Holy Spirit. Gift of God.

TEARS: Emotional sowing; mostly distress but could represent brokenness. Joy.

Tea

TEETH: Wisdom, gaining understanding; to work something out.

> *Baby teeth*: Childish. Without wisdom or knowledge.
>
> *Broken teeth*: Inexperienced. Difficulty in coming to understanding.
>
> *Brushing teeth*: Gaining wisdom or understanding.
>
> *False teeth:* Full of reasoning of this world instead of pure spiritual understanding.
>
> *Toothache*: Tribulation coming; heartache.

TELEPHONE: Spiritual communication, good or evil. Godly counsel.

TELESCOPE: Looking or planning for the future. To make a problem appear bigger and closer.

Telephone

TELEVISION: Visionary revelations or prophetic dreams. Prophetic utterance.

TEMPLE: A place of meeting with God. A place of refuge. God's habitation. Human body.

TEN: Law, government order and obligation. Testing trial.

TENT: Temporary covering. Flexible.

TEN Thousand: Army of the Lord. Battle readiness.

Tent

> *And he said: "The Lord came from Sinai, and dawned on them from Seir; He shone forth from Mount Paran, and He came with ten thousands of saints; from His right hand came a fiery law for them"* (Deuteronomy 33:2 NKJ).

> *Now Enoch, the seventh from Adam, prophesied about these men also, saying, "Behold, the Lord comes with ten thousands of His saints"* (Jude 1:14 NKJ).

TERMITES: Something that can cause hidden destruction.

THIEF: Satan. Deceiver. Secret intruder. Unexpected loss.

THIGH: Strength; flesh. To entice. Oath taken.

THIRTEEN: Rebellion; backsliding.

THIRTY: Beginning of ministry. Mature for God's work. Jesus was thirty when He began His ministry; Joseph was thirty when he became prime minister.

THORNS: Evil disturbance. Curse. Gossip.

THOUSANDS: Maturity approved.

THREE/THIRD: Witness; divine fullness; Godhead. Triumph over sin. Resurrection. Conform.

THREE HUNDRED: Chosen by God. Reserve of the Lord.

> *The Lord said to Gideon, "With the three hundred men that lapped I will save you and give the Midianites into your hands. Let all the other men go, each to his own place." So Gideon sent the rest of the Israelites to their tents but kept the three hundred, who took over the provisions and trumpets of the others. Now the camp of Midian lay below him in the valley* (Judges 7:7-8).

THRONE: A seat of power. A place of authority. God's throne. Evil throne.

> *At once I was in the Spirit, and there before me was a throne in heaven with someone sitting on it. And the one who sat there had the appearance of jasper and carnelian. A rainbow, resembling an emerald, encircled the throne"* (Revelation 4:2-3).

THUMB: Apostolic; authority; soul power.

THUNDER: Loud signal from God. God speaking, touching. Warning or blessing.

TIN: Something of low valor. Not original, an imitation.

TITANIC: Big plan that is not going to work out.

TITLE/DEED: Ownership seal. Potential to possess something.

TONGUE: Powerful. National language. Something that cann' tamed.

TORNADO: Distressing situation. Great trouble. Spiritual warfare.

TOWER: High spiritual thing. Supernatural experience. Great strength. Pride, i.e. the tower of Babel.

TRACTOR: Groundbreaking ministry. Prepare the mind to receive.

Trailer: An equipping ministry. A caring service. A ministry that is migrating.

TRAIN: A large ministry that influences a lot of people. Move or send people out. Movement of God.

TREE: Leader, good or bad. Person or organization. Nations or kingdom.

Christmas: Celebrations.

Evergreen: Long-lasting, everlasting.

Oak: Great strength. Durable.

Olive: Anointed of God. Israel. Church. Anointing oil.

Palm: A leader that is fruit producing.

Tree stump: Tenacity or stubbornness. Retaining hope despite circumstances. Keeping the root in place.

Willow: Indicating sadness; defeat.

And provide for those who grieve in Zion—to bestow on them a crown of beauty instead of ashes, the oil of gladness instead of mourning, and a garment of praise instead of a spirit of despair. They will be called oaks of righteousness, a planting of the Lord for the display of His splendor (Isaiah 61:3).

These are the visions I saw while lying in my bed: I looked, and there before me stood a tree in the middle of the land. Its height was enormous (Daniel 4:10).

A shoot will come up from the stump of Jesse; from his roots a Branch will bear fruit (Isaiah 11:1).

But let the stump and its roots, bound with iron and bronze, remain in ... the grass of the field. Let him be drenched with the dew ... let him live with the animals among the plants of the ... (:15).

... be ...

1 ministry that brings provision.

TRUMPET: Voice of the prophet. The second coming of Christ. Proclaiming the good news. Blessing; promise.

> *To gather the assembly, blow the trumpets, but not with the same signal* (Numbers 10:7).

> *For the Lord Himself will come down from heaven, with a loud command, with the voice of the archangel and with the trumpet call of God, and the dead in Christ will rise first* (1 Thessalonians 4:16).

TUNNEL: A passage. A time or place of transition. Troubled or dark seasons of life.

> *He tunnels through the rock; his eyes see all its treasures* (Job 28:10).

TWELVE: Government of God. Divine order. Discipleship. Government by election, theocracy.

TWENTY: Holiness and redemption.

TWENTY-FOUR: Completed order of God. Maturity; perfect government. Elders in the throne room.

> *Surrounding the throne were twenty-four other thrones, and seated on them were twenty four elders. They were dressed in white and had crowns of gold on their heads* (Revelation 4:4).

TWO: Witnessing; confirmation. Division. Whole in marriage.

TWO HUNDRED: Fullness confirmed. Promise guaranteed.

TWO STORY: Multilevel giftedness. Symbolic of flesh and spirit. Multitalented church.

UPSTAIRS: Pertaining to the Spirit. Pentecost. Zone of thought; great balance. Spiritual realm.

UPWARD MOTION: Moving onto higher spiritual things.

URINATING: Releasing pressure. Compelling urge or temptation. Repentance.

VAN, MOVING: A time or period of change, either in the natural or in the spirit. To walk.

VAPOR: Something temporary. Presence of God. Evidence of something.

VEIL: To conceal. To conceal glory or sin. To deceive. Blind to the truth. Lack of understanding.

Even to this day when Moses is read, a veil covers their hearts. But whenever anyone turns to the Lord, the veil is taken away (2 Corinthians 3:15-16).

And even if our gospel is veiled, it is veiled to those who are perishing (2 Corinthians 4:3).

VESSEL: People as instrument of use, for good or bad purposes. The Christian believers.

VINE: Jesus Christ. Christian believers.

I had planted you like a choice vine of sound and reliable stock. How then did you turn against Me into a corrupt, wild vine? (Jeremiah 2:21)

I am the true vine, and My Father is the gardener (John 15:1).

VINEYARD: A place of planting; harvest. Heavenly Kingdom.

The vineyard of the Lord Almighty is the house of Israel, and the men of Judah are the garden of His delight. And He looked for justice, but saw bloodshed; for righteousness, but heard cries of distress (Isaiah 5:7).

VOICE: Message from God or devil. The Word of God. Godly instruction.

VOLCANO: Something sudden and explosive. Out of control and unstable; unpredictable. Judgment.

WALKING: Walking the path of life; life in the Spirit. Progress, living in the Spirit.

Difficulty: Trials or opposition; evil opposition to destiny.

Unable: Hindrance to doing what you are called to do.

WALL: Obstacle, barrier, defense, limitation. Great hindrance. Blocking the view of presenting spiritual signs.

WAR: Spiritual warfare.

WASHING: To clean.

WASHBASIN: Means of cleansing. Prayers and intercession.

WASHCLOTH: Something that enhances the cleansing process.

WATCH: Need to be watchful. Time for something. Watch what's about to happen.

WATERMELON: Spirit-ruled soul. Fruitfulness.

WATERS: Move of the Spirit; Holy Spirit. Nations of the world.

Stagnant: Instability.

Muddy or polluted: Corrupted spiritual moves, sin, false doctrine.

Troubled water: Healing pool. Troubled mind.

Water fountain: God's Spirit welling up in man. Salvation. Revival coming. Time of refreshing.

WEEDS: Sinful nature or acts.

WEIGHT: Great responsibility, load, or burden.

WHEEL: Pertaining to life cycle. Long-lasting. Continuously.

WHIRLWIND: Powerful move in the spirit, good or bad.

WHITE: Something that is pure, righteousness. God's glory, light of God. Innocence, blamelessness.

WIFE: Actual person. Someone joined to you in covenant. Spirit of submission. The Church. Israel. The work of Christ in the dreamer.

WILDERNESS: Hard times. Place of trial/testing. Distant from God. Place of training. Place of provision.

WIND, BLOWING: Movement of the spirit, usually good, but may be evil. Disappears quickly. Unstable. Difficult to understand.

WINDOW: Prophetic gifting. Revelation knowledge. Gaining insight.

WINE: Holy Spirit. Counterfeit spirit. Communion. Teaching; blessing.

Then I will send rain on your land in its season, both autumn and spring rains, so that you may gather in your grain, new wine and oil (Deuteronomy 11:14).

No, new wine must be poured into new wineskins (Luke 5:38).

Likewise, teach the older women to be reverent in the way they live, not to be slanderers or addicted to much wine, but to teach what is good (Titus 2:3).

WINEPRESS: True doctrine.

WINESKINS: The Body. The Church.

WINGS: Prophetic. Under the protection of God.

You yourselves have seen what I did to Egypt, and how I carried you on eagles' wings and brought you to Myself (Exodus 19:4).

Have mercy on me, O God, have mercy on me, for in You my soul takes refuge. I will take refuge in the shadow of Your wings until the disaster has passed (Psalm 57:1).

Each of the four living creatures had six wings and was covered with eyes all around, even under his wings. Day and night they never stop saying: "Holy, holy, holy is the Lord God Almighty, who was, and is, and is to come" (Revelation 4:8).

O Jerusalem, Jerusalem, you who kill the prophets and stone those sent to you, how often I have longed to gather your children together, as a hen gathers her chicks under her wings, but you were not willing! (Luke 13:34)

WINTER: Season of unfruitfulness. Latent period.

Pray that your flight will not take place in winter or on the Sabbath (Matthew 24:20).

Do your best to get here before winter. Eubulus greets you, and so do Pudens, Linus, Claudia and all the brothers (2 Timothy 4:21).

WITCH: Spirit of rebellion. Non-submission. Manipulative person. Spirit of control.

For rebellion is as the sin of witchcraft (1 Samuel 15:23a NKJ).

WOLF: A tendency to destroy God's work. False minister. Opportunistic person.

WOMAN (UNKNOWN): A messenger from God or satan. An angel or demonic spirit. Seducing spirit.

WOOD: Life. Dependence on flesh. Humanity. Carnal reasoning. Lust.

WORK Area: The place or time of your service.

WORM: Something that eats from the inside, often secretly. Not obvious on the surface. Disease; filthiness.

WRESTLING: Struggling with something in the spirit or real life. To battle. Perseverance. To contend with, struggle.

YARD: The opened part of your personality. Behind or past.

YEAR: Time of blessing or judgment.

YELLOW: Hope; fear; mind.

YOKE: Bondage. Tied to something; usually evil but sometimes good. Enslaved.

ZION: A place of strength. A place of protection. God's Kingdom.

Here am I, and the children the Lord has given me. We are signs and symbols in Israel from the Lord Almighty, who dwells on Mount Zion (Isaiah 8:18).

Their bloodguilt, which I have not pardoned, I will pardon. The Lord dwells in Zion! (Joel 3:21).

But on Mount Zion will be deliverance; it will be holy, and the house of Jacob will possess its inheritance (Obadiah 1:17).

PART 3

OTHER
Symbolic
OVERTONES

ACTIONS AND FEELINGS

FEELINGS OR EMOTIONS: Feelings in dreams are expressions of what the truest situation is in the life of the dreamer. They come without the moderating effect of social norms, mind-sets, prejudices, or pretences. Sometimes, the feeling expressed by the dreamer may be incongruous to what the dreamer thinks he or she is. If this happens, it is often because there are suppressed desires or hidden hurts, wounds, or scars in the life of the dreamer that could resurrect. By and large, most feelings in dreams are usually the reflection of the degree or intensity with which an actual event will eventually happen. However, in my experience, in over 80 percent of cases, the following feelings are symbolized as indicated below.

Anger: Anger.

Bitterness: Bitterness.

Hatred: Hatred.

Joy: Happiness.

Love: Love.

Sadness: Lack of joy.

Tears: Deep emotional move, could either be for a pleasant or unpleasant reason.

FLYING: The dreamer has the potential to soar high in the things of the Spirit. Divine miraculous intervention, especially the provision of escape from danger or acceleration towards destiny.

HUNGRY: Inspiration to desire spiritual food. Lack of adequate spiritual nourishment.

INABILITY TO MOVE: This may indicate hindrances to the divine purposes in the life of the dreamer. Call for intensification of spiritual warfare.

INDIFFERENT: Not considerate. Resistant. Perseverance. Carefree.

RUNNING: (Consider the context of the dream.) Accelerated pace of events is approaching—either towards or away from something.

SLEEP: To be overtaken by something beyond your control.

THINKING: A time of study, reflection, meditation, and intellectual exercise.

WALKING: The normal routine or run of life events; the expected pace of progression.

On gravel, on stones: Hard times.

On sand: May indicate not having sound foundation on the aspect of life the dream addresses.

On swampy, moldy path: May indicate sticky situation, hard times, or hindrances.

On clear waters: Moving in the Spirit and grace of God.

On dirty waters: Dabbling in wrong doctrines.

On a straight path with near infinite view: Many places to go in life.

WORRYING: Uncertain times, insecurity. Consider the context of its occurrence.

SCHOOLS/SCHOOLING

*Note the level of school education in the dream.

SCHOOL BUILDING: May indicate a place of learning, church, or professional institute.

PRIMARY SCHOOL: Indicates the fundamental things of life.

SECONDARY SCHOOL: Indicates the equipping period of life.

TERTIARY SCHOOL: Indicates the definite place of specialized call on the dreamer's life.

HIGH SCHOOL: Moving into a higher level of walk with God. Capable of giving same to others.

DELAY/HINDRANCES OR DISTURBANCES DURING EXAMINATIONS: May be indications of negative influences that are at play in deciding the desired placement. It could represent personal weaknesses that are standing in the way of the dreamer.

END OF SCHOOL SEASON: Indicates the completion of the equipping season.

EXAMINATION: At the verge of a promotion.

FAILING EXAMINATIONS: May mean one is not meeting the requirement for the desired placement.

INABILITY TO GET TO THE SCHOOL PREMISES: Indicates you are not in the right place for the required equipping. Extraneous hindrances to the dreamer's drive to achieve required equipping.

INABILITY TO LOCATE A CLASSROOM: May indicate inner uncertainty about definite vocation or call of God in the dreamer.

LATENESS: May indicate inadequate preparation for a time of equipping.

OLD SCHOOL TIME OR PLACE: May indicate similar time or season of experience and importance is at hand or imminent.

NOT FINISHING A TEST: Could mean inadequate preparation.

PASSING EXAMINATIONS: Confirms divine approval for the promotion.

PREPARING FOR EXAMINATION: A season preceding a promotion.

RECEIVING OR GIVING A LECTURE: The theme of the lecture is the message for the dreamer, or for the people or occasion.

RUNNING OUT OF PAPER, INK, OR PEN: Could indicate inadequate knowledge for the desired placement.

Parts of the Human Body

BEARD: To have respect for authority.

So Hanun seized David's men, shaved off half of each man's beard, cut off their garments in the middle at the buttocks, and sent them away. When David was told about this, he sent messengers to meet the men, for they were greatly humiliated. The king said, "Stay at Jericho till your beards have grown, and then come back" (2 Samuel 10:4-5).

Messy: Insanity.

Trimmed: Respectable or sane.

BELLY: Feelings, desires. Spiritual well-being. Sentiment. Humiliation.

They conceive trouble and give birth to evil; their womb [belly] *fashions deceit* (Job 15:35).

Whoever believes in Me, as the Scripture has said, streams of living water will flow from within [from his belly] *him* (John 7:38).

For such people are not serving our Lord Christ, but their own [belly] *appetites. By smooth talk and flattery they deceive the minds of naive people* (Romans 16:18).

BONES: The substance of something. The main issue. Long lasting.

Moses took the bones of Joseph with him because Joseph had made the sons of Israel swear an oath. He had said, "God will surely come to your aid, and then you must carry my bones up with you from this place" (Exodus 13:19).

Once while some Israelites were burying a man, suddenly they saw a band of raiders; so they threw the man's body into Elisha's tomb. When the body touched Elisha's bones, the man came to life and stood up on his feet (2 Kings 13:21).

BONES, SKELETON: Something without substance or flesh. Something without details.

EYES: The means of seeing. To want something. The seer's anointing.

Closed eyes: Spiritual blindness. Ignorance, mostly self-imposed.

Winking: Concealed intention or cunning person.

FACE: Who the person is. The identity of the person. The reflection of the heart of the person. Identity or characteristics. Image expression.

FEET: Symbol of the heart or thought pattern. The part of the body that comes in contact with the earth. The lower members of the Church. Not to be ignored. Have tendency to be ignored.

And with your feet fitted with the readiness that comes from the gospel of peace (Ephesians 6:15).

"Do not come any closer," God said. "Take off your sandals, for the place where you are standing is holy ground" (Exodus 3:5).

If the foot should say, "Because I am not a hand, I do not belong to the body," it would not for that reason cease to be part of the body (1 Corinthians 12:15).

Bare foot: Humble before the presence of God. Lack of studying the Word of God. Lack of preparation.

Diseased: Spirit of offense.

Lame feet: Crippled with unbelief, mind-set. Negative stronghold.

Kicking: Not under authority or working against authority.

Overgrown nails: Lack of care or not in proper order.

Washing: Humility or Christian duty.

FINGERS: Image of activity, whether human or divine. Image of sensitivity. Denoting power or authority. Assigning blame. Unit of measure. For battle.

Then Pharaoh took his signet ring from his finger and put it on Joseph's finger. He dressed him in robes of fine linen and put a gold chain around his neck (Genesis 41:42).

The magicians said to Pharaoh, "This is the finger of God." But Pharaoh's heart was hard and he would not listen, just as the Lord had said (Exodus 8:19).

Then you will call, and the Lord will answer; you will cry for help, and He will say: Here am I. If you do away with the yoke of oppression, with the pointing finger and malicious talk (Isaiah 58:9).

For your hands are stained with blood, your fingers with guilt. Your lips have spoken lies, and your tongue mutters wicked things (Isaiah 59:3).

Each of the pillars was eighteen cubits high and twelve cubits in circumference; each was four fingers thick, and hollow (Jeremiah 52:21).

The young men who had grown up with him replied, "Tell these people who have said to you, 'Your father put a heavy yoke on us, but make our yoke lighter'—tell them, 'My little finger is thicker than my father's waist'" (1 Kings 12:10).

Praise be to the Lord my Rock, who trains my hands for war, my fingers for battle (Psalm 144:1).

Clenched: Pride or boastfulness.

Finger of God: Work of God or authority of God.

Fourth: Teacher.

Index: Prophet.

Little: Pastor.

Middle: Evangelist.

Pointed finger: Accusations or persecutions. Instruction or direction.

Thumb: Apostle.

FOREHEAD: That which is prominent and determines the identity of something or someone.

Therefore the showers have been withheld, and there has been no latter rain. You have had a harlot's forehead; you refuse to be ashamed (Jeremiah 3:3 NKJ).

They will see His face, and His name will be on their foreheads (Revelation 22:4).

HAIR: Cover, or something numerous, or man's glory. Protection, beauty, and identification. Mark of beauty or pride. Uncut hair is symbol of covenant. Long hair is a shame for men but glory for women. Sign of good age or dignity.

Whenever he cut the hair of his head—he used to cut his hair from time to time when it became too heavy for him—he would weigh it, and its weight was two hundred shekels by the royal standard (2 Samuel 14:26).

Because you will conceive and give birth to a son. No razor may be used on his head, because the boy is to be a Nazirite, set apart to God from birth, and he will begin the deliverance of Israel from the hands of the Philistines (Judges 13:5).

Does not the very nature of things teach you that if a man has long hair, it is a disgrace to him, but that if a woman has long hair, it is her glory? For long hair is given to her as a covering. If anyone wants to be contentious about this, we have no other practice—nor do the churches of God (1 Corinthians 11:14-16).

As I looked, thrones were set in place, and the Ancient of Days took His seat. His clothing was as white as snow; the Hair of his head was white like wool. His throne was flaming with fire, and its wheels were all ablaze (Daniel 7:9).

Grey hair is a crown of splendor; it is attained by a righteous life (Proverbs 16:31).

Baldness: Grief and shame.

Haircut: Getting something in correct shape or cutting off evil or bad habit or tradition.

Long and well maintained: Covenant and strength.

Long on a man: Probably rebellious behavior or covenant relationship.

Long on a woman: Glory of womanhood. Wife or submissive church.

Long and unkempt: Out of control.

Losing hair: Loss of wisdom or glory.

Out of shape: Not in order.

Shaving: Getting rid of things that hinder or things that are dirty.

Short on a woman: Probably lack of submission or manliness.

HANDS: Power. Personal service, taking action on behalf of someone. A person in action. Means of service. Means of expressing strength.

The fear and dread of you will fall upon all the beasts of the earth and all the birds of the air, upon every creature that moves along the ground, and upon all the fish of the sea; they are given into your hands (Genesis 9:2).

So they called together all the rulers of the Philistines and said, "Send the ark of the god of Israel away; let it go back to its own place, or it will kill us and our people." For death had filled the city with panic; God's hand was very heavy upon it (1 Samuel 5:11).

My Father, who has given them to Me, is greater than all; no one can snatch them out of My Father's hand (John 10:29).

Stretch out your hand to heal and perform miraculous signs and wonders through the name of your holy servant Jesus (Acts 4:30).

The Lord rewards every man for his righteousness and faithfulness. The Lord delivered you into my hands today, but I would not lay a hand on the Lord's anointed (1 Samuel 26:23).

The Lord says to my Lord: "Sit at my right hand until I make your enemies a footstool for your feet" (Psalm 110:1).

But Israel reached out his right hand and put it on Ephraim's head, though he was the younger, and crossing his arms, he put his left hand on Manasseh's head, even though Manasseh was the firstborn (Genesis 48:14).

Do not neglect your gift, which was given you through a prophetic message when the body of elders laid their hands on you (1 Timothy 4:14).

For this reason I remind you to fan into flame the gift of God, which is in you through the laying on of my hands (2 Timothy 1:6).

Clapping: Joy and worship.

Fist: Pride in one's strength.

Covering face: Anger. Guilt or shame.

Holding: In agreement.

Left hand: Something spiritual.

Place on the right hand: Position of honor.

Put hand on the head: Blessings. Ordination.

Raised: Surrender or worshipping.

Right hand: Oath of allegiance; means of power of honor, natural strengths.

Shaking hands: Coming to an agreement. Surrender.

Stretched out hands: In security or anger.

Striking: Demonstrating strength or anger.

Trembling: To fear; spirit of fear; anxiety/awe at God's presence.

Under thighs: In oaths.

Washing: Declaring innocence or to dissociate oneself.

HEAD: Leader. To take responsibility. Be proud of something. God-ordained authority—husband. Christ. Christ as head of all people. God as the Father and head of Christ.

And Moses chose able men out of all Israel, and made them heads over the people: rulers of thousands, rulers of hundreds, rulers of fifties, and rulers of tens (Exodus 18:25 NKJ).

If anyone goes outside your house into the street, his blood will be on his own head; we will not be responsible. As for anyone who is in the house with you, his blood will be on our head if a hand is laid on him (Joshua 2:19).

Now I want you to realize that the head of every man is Christ, and the head of the woman is man, and the head of Christ is God (1 Corinthians 11:3).

For the husband is the head of the wife as Christ is the head of the church, His body, of which He is the Savior (Ephesians 5:23).

Instead, speaking the truth in love, we will in all things grow up into Him who is the Head, that is, Christ (Ephesians 4:15).

And He is the head of the body, the church; He is the beginning and the firstborn from among the dead, so that in everything He might have the supremacy (Colossians 1:18).

He has lost connection with the Head, from whom the whole body, supported and held together by its ligaments and sinews, grows as God causes it to grow (Colossians 2:19).

And you have been given fullness in Christ, who is the head over every power and authority (Colossians 2:10).

Anointed: Set apart for God's service.

Covered with the hand: Signifying sorrow.

HEART: Most mentioning of the heart in Scripture is almost never in literal terms. The seat of affection. The seat of intellect. Innermost being.

Do not trust in extortion or take pride in stolen goods; though your riches increase, do not set your heart on them (Psalm 62:10).

The Lord saw how great man's wickedness on the earth had become, and that every inclination of the thoughts of his heart was only evil all the time (Genesis: 6:5).

Blessed are they who keep His statutes and seek Him with all their heart (Psalm 119:2).

The Lord was grieved that He had made man on the earth, and His heart was filled with pain (Genesis 6:6).

HEEL: The crushing power.

HIPS: Reproduction. Relating to reproduction or supporting structure.

KNEES: Sign of expression of relationship. Submission, blessing, or fear. Submission to Christ. Blessing. A measure of faith.

> *Then, at the evening sacrifice, I rose from my self-abasement, with my tunic and cloak torn, and fell on my knees with my hands spread out to the Lord my God* (Ezra 9:5).

> *That at the name of Jesus every knee should bow, in heaven and on earth and under the earth, and every tongue confess that Jesus Christ is Lord, to the glory of God the Father* (Philippians 2:10-11).

> *Why were there knees to receive me and breasts that I might be nursed?* (Job 3:12)

> *Your words have supported those who stumbled; you have strengthened faltering knees* (Job 4:4).

> *They are brought to their knees and fall, but we rise up and stand firm* (Psalm 20:8).

> *Strengthen the feeble hands, steady the knees that give way* (Isaiah 35:3).

> **Trembling knees:** Weakness or fear.

LEGS: Means of support. Spiritual strength to walk in life. Symbol of strength. Object of beauty. Something you stand on—your foundational principles.

> *His pleasure is not in the strength of the horse, nor His delight in the legs of a man* (Psalm 147:10).

> *Then I saw another mighty angel coming down from heaven. He was robed in a cloud, with a rainbow above his head; his face was like the sun, and his legs were like fiery pillars* (Revelation 10:1).

> *His legs are pillars of marble set on bases of pure gold. His appearance is like Lebanon, choice as its cedars* (Song 5:15).

> *How beautiful your sandaled feet, O prince's daughter! Your graceful legs are like jewels, the work of a craftsman's hands* (Song 7:1).

> *His face turned pale and he was so frightened that his knees knocked together and his legs gave way* (Daniel 5:6).

> *I heard and my heart pounded, my lips quivered at the sound; decay crept into my bones, and my legs trembled. Yet I will wait patiently for the day of calamity to come on the nation invading us* (Habakkuk 3:16).

> **Legs giving way:** Giving up on the issue.

> **Female legs:** Power to entice.

LIPS: Reflects the quality of the heart. Lying lips. Can determine outcome in life. Issuing deception. Object of seduction.

Let their lying lips be silenced, for with pride and contempt they speak arrogantly against the righteous (Psalm 31:18).

He who guards his lips guards his life, but he who speaks rashly will come to ruin (Proverbs 13:3).

Words from a wise man's mouth are gracious, but a fool is consumed by his own lips (Ecclesiastes 10:12).

The Lord says: "These people come near to Me with their mouth and honor Me with their lips, but their hearts are far from Me. Their worship of Me is made up only of rules taught by men (Isaiah 29:13).

His cheeks are like beds of spice yielding perfume. His lips are like lilies dripping with myrrh (Song 5:13).

MOUTH: Instrument of witnessing. Speaking evil or good words. Something from which comes the issues of life. Words coming against you.

NECK: Associated with beauty. A place to secure something valuable. Capture and subjection. Cut off or break.

Outstretched: Arrogance.

Long neck: Noisy.

Risk the neck: To take risk.

Stiff-necked: Stubbornness.

Are they not finding and dividing the spoils: a girl or two for each man, colorful garments as plunder for Sisera, colorful garments embroidered, highly embroidered garments for my neck—all this as plunder? (Judges 5:30)

They will be a garland to grace your head and a chain to adorn your neck (Proverbs 1:9).

Let love and faithfulness never leave you; bind them around your neck, write them on the tablet of your heart (Proverbs 3:3).

In His great power God becomes like clothing to me; He binds me like the neck of my garment (Job 30:18).

The Lord has appointed you priest in place of Jehoiada to be in charge of the house of the Lord ; you should put any madman who acts like a prophet into the stocks and neck-irons (Jeremiah 29:26).

Therefore in hunger and thirst, in nakedness and dire poverty, you will serve the enemies the Lord sends against you. He will put an iron yoke on your neck until He has destroyed you (Deuteronomy 28:48).

Who risked their own necks for my life, to whom not only I give thanks, but also all the churches of the Gentiles (Romans 16:4 NKJ).

NOSE: Discerning spirit. Discernment, good or bad. Intruding into people's privacy. Gossiper.

SHOULDERS: The responsibility, the authority. Something, person or animal on which burden or load is laid or can be placed. Something that can be of good for work. Governmental responsibility. Sign of unity – shoulder to shoulder. Captivity.

For as in the day of Midian's defeat, you have shattered the yoke that burdens them, the bar across their shoulders, the rod of their oppressor (Isaiah 9:4).

For to us a child is born, to us a son is given, and the government will be on His shoulders. And He will be called Wonderful Counselor, Mighty God, Everlasting Father, Prince of Peace (Isaiah 9:6).

Then will I purify the lips of the peoples, that all of them may call on the name of the Lord and serve Him shoulder to shoulder (Zephaniah 3:9).

He says, "I removed the burden from their shoulders; their hands were set free from the basket" (Psalm 81:6).

They tie up heavy loads and put them on men's shoulders, but they themselves are not willing to lift a finger to move them (Matthew 23:4).

Bare female shoulders: Enticement.

Broad: Capable of handling much responsibility.

Drooped: Defeated attitude, overworked, overtired, burnt-out.

TEETH: Primary symbol of strength. Image of good consumption by breaking down into tiny bits. To simplify into its smallest bits for easy processing for wisdom. Power.

And there before me was a second beast, which looked like a bear. It was raised up on one of its sides, and it had three ribs in its mouth between its teeth. It was told, "Get up and eat your fill of flesh!" (Daniel 7:5)

Like the ungodly they maliciously mocked; they gnashed their teeth at me (Psalm 35:16).

But the subjects of the kingdom will be thrown outside, into the darkness, where there will be weeping and gnashing of teeth (Matthew 8:12).

Baby teeth*:* Immaturity.

Breaking of teeth: Defeat and/or losing wisdom.

Brushing teeth: Gaining understanding.

False teeth: Wisdom of this world.

Gnashing of teeth: Sign of taunt, division or regret and sorrow.

Toothache: Trial, problems.

BUILDINGS

Personalities or Structure of an Organization

I will show you what he is like who comes to Me and hears My words and puts them into practice. He is like a man building a house, who dug down deep and laid the foundation on rock. When the flood came, the torrent struck that house but could not shake it, because it was well built (Luke 6:47-48).

CHURCH BUILDING: Pertaining to church, ministry, or the call of God.

COURTROOM: Being judged. Under scrutiny. Persecution, trial.

CURRENT HOUSE: The dreamer's make-up.

FACTORY: A place of putting things together. A place of protection. A church.

Foundation: Something on which the person or object stands on.

Idle: Not put into proper use.

Factory in good state: Good standing.

Factory ruins: Needing attention.

FAMILY HOME: Related to the past. Something from the past influencing the present. Something from the bloodline.

House:

High-rise: Multitalented ministry; multiple ministries in one place.

Mobile home: A transitory situation. Character in transition. Temporary place.

Moving home: Changes in personality.

New: New personality, either natural or spiritual.

Old: Past or something inherited. If in good state, then it is righteous or good from the past. If in bad state, then it is sin or weakness that runs in a family.

Shop: A place of choices. Business related venue.

Under construction: In process of formation.

LIBRARY: Time or place of knowledge; education.

OFFICE BUILDING: Relates to secular jobs, the dreamer's office life.

Parts of a Building

BACK: Something in the past or unexpected.

BATHROOM: A period of cleansing; entering a time of repentance. A place of voluntary nakedness. Facing reality in individual life.

BEDROOM: A place of intimacy. A place of rest or where you sleep and dream. A place of covenant or a place of revelation.

FRONT: Something in the future.

KITCHEN: A plea of nourishment; heart. The mind or intellect, where ideas are muted in the natural realm. The heart (Spirit). Where revelations are received and nurtured for the equipping of others.

ROOF: The covering.

SITTING ROOM: That which is easily noticed by the public. The revealed part.

States of a Building

CRACKED WALL: Faulty protective measures. Not adequately protected.

LEAKING ROOF: Inadequate spiritual cover.

MODERN: Current doctrine up-to-date.

NEGLECTED: Lack of maintenance.

OLD-FASHIONED: Tradition or old belief.

SPIRITUAL SIGNIFICANCE OF NUMBERS

God speaks through numbers a great deal, and the Bible is full of evidence of God's arithmetic. Numbers are high-level forms of symbolism. I have put together some numbers and their generally accepted scriptural relevance or meaning. The spiritual significance of numbers given here is based on the Word of God, and I have found it very useful in my personal experience.

ONE: Unity. The number of God. The beginning, the first. Precious.

> *There is one body and one Spirit—just as you were called to one hope when you were called—one Lord, one faith, one baptism; one God and Father of all, who is over all and through all and in all* (Ephesians 4:4-6).

> *I and the Father are one* (John 10:30).

> *That all of them may be one, Father, just as You are in Me and I am in You. May they also be in Us so that the world may believe that You have sent Me. I have given them the glory that You gave Me, that they may be one as We are one* (John 17:21-22).

> *Make every effort to keep the unity of the Spirit through the bond of peace* (Ephesians 4:3).

> *And I will pour out on the house of David and the inhabitants of Jerusalem a spirit of grace and supplication. They will look on Me, the one they have pierced, and they will mourn for Him as one mourns for an only child, and grieve bitterly for Him as one grieves for a firstborn son* (Zechariah 12:10).

> *A mediator, however, does not represent just one party; but God is one* (Galatians 3:20).

TWO: Union, witnessing or confirmation. It could also mean division depending on the general context of the events or revelation.

> *The man said, "This is now bone of my bones and flesh of my flesh; she shall be called 'woman,' for she was taken out of man." For this reason a man will leave his father and mother and be united to his wife, and they will become one flesh* (Genesis 2:23-24).

But if he will not listen, take one or two others along, so that every matter may be established by the testimony of two or three witnesses (Matthew 18:16).

He is a double-minded man, unstable in all he does (James 1:8).

So God made the expanse and separated the water under the expanse from the water above it. And it was so. God called the expanse "sky." And there was evening, and there was morning—the second day (Genesis 1:7-8).

Then the king said, "Bring me a sword." So they brought a sword for the king. He then gave an order: "Cut the living child in two and give half to one and half to the other" (1 Kings 3:24-25).

THREE: Resurrection, divine completeness and perfection. Confirmation. The trinity of Godhead. Restoration.

Therefore go and make disciples of all nations, baptizing them in the name of the Father and of the Son and of the Holy Spirit (Matthew 28:19).

For as Jonah was three days and three nights in the belly of a huge fish, so the Son of Man will be three days and three nights in the heart of the earth (Matthew 12:40).

Jesus answered them, "Destroy this temple, and I will raise it again in three days" (John 2:19).

FOUR: Creation or to rule or to reign. On the fourth day of creation, God made two great lights—the sun and the moon—to rule the day and the night.

And God said, "Let there be lights in the expanse of the sky to separate the day from the night, and let them serve as signs to mark seasons and days and years, and let them be lights in the expanse of the sky to give light on the earth." And it was so. God made two great lights—the greater light to govern the day and the lesser light to govern the night. He also made the stars. God set them in the expanse of the sky to give light on the earth, to govern the day and the night, and to separate light from darkness. And God saw that it was good. And there was evening, and there was morning—the fourth day (Genesis 1:14-19).

Also before the throne there was what looked like a sea of glass, clear as crystal. In the center, around the throne, were four living creatures, and they were covered with eyes, in front and in back. The first living creature was like a lion, the second was like an ox, the third had a face like a man, the fourth was like a flying eagle. Each of the four living creatures had six wings and was covered with eyes all around, even under his wings. Day and night they never stop saying: 'Holy, holy, holy is the Lord God Almighty, who was, and is, and is to come" (Revelation 4:6-8).

FIVE: Grace or the goodness of God. Fivefold ministry.

It was He who gave some to be apostles, some to be prophets, some to be evangelists, and some to be pastors and teachers (Ephesians 4:11).

SIX: The number of man. Weakness of humanity or the flesh. Can mean evil or satan. God created man on the sixth day.

Then God said, "Let us make man in Our image, in Our likeness, and let them rule over the fish of the sea and the birds of the air, over the livestock, over all the earth, and over all the creatures that move along the ground." So God created man in His own image, in the image of God He created him; male and female He created them (Genesis 1:26-27).

Nebuchadnezzar the king made an image of gold, whose height was sixty cubits and its width six cubits. He set it up in the plain of Dura, in the province of Babylon (Daniel 3:1 NKJ).

SEVEN: Completeness or spiritual perfection. Rest. Blessing. Redemption.

Thus the heavens and the earth were completed in all their vast array. By the seventh day God had finished the work He had been doing; so on the seventh day He rested from all His work. And God blessed the seventh day and made it holy, because on it He rested from all the work of creating that He had done (Genesis 2:1-3).

But in the days when the seventh angel is about to sound his trumpet, the mystery of God will be accomplished, just as He announced to His servants the prophets (Revelation 10:7).

The seventh angel poured out his bowl into the air, and out of the temple came a loud voice from the throne, saying, "It is done!" (Revelation 16:17)

At the end of every seven years you must cancel debts. This is how it is to be done: Every creditor shall cancel the loan he has made to his fellow Israelite. He shall not require payment from his fellow Israelite or brother, because the Lord's time for cancelling debts has been proclaimed (Deuteronomy 15:1-2).

EIGHT: New birth or new beginning. The circumcision of male children of Israel on the eighth day is a type of new birth.

*On the eighth day, when it was time to circumcise Him, He was named
Jesus, the name the angel had given Him before He had been conceived.
When the time of their purification according to the Law of Moses had
been completed, Joseph and Mary took Him to Jerusalem to present Him
to the Lord (as it is written in the Law of the Lord, "Every firstborn male
is to be consecrated to the Lord")* (Luke 2:21-23).

*For the generations to come every male among you who is eight days
old must be circumcised, including those born in your household or
bought with money from a foreigner—those who are not your offspring* (Genesis 17:12).

NINE: Fruit of the Spirit. Harvest or the fruit of your labor. Nine gifts
of the Spirit.

*But the fruit of the Spirit is love, joy, peace, patience, kindness, good-
ness, faithfulness, gentleness and self-control. Against such things
there is no law* (Galatians 5:22-23).

*To one there is given through the Spirit the message of wisdom, to
another the message of knowledge by means of the same Spirit, to
another faith by the same Spirit, to another gifts of healing by that
one Spirit, to another miraculous powers, to another prophecy, to
another distinguishing between spirits, to another speaking in different
kinds of tongues, and to still another the interpretation of tongues* (1
Corinthians 12:8-10).

TEN: Law and responsibility. Tithe is a tenth of our earning, which
belongs to God. It is also the number for the pastoral. Judgment. Ten
plagues upon Egypt.

ELEVEN: Confusion, judgment, or disorder.

TWELVE: Government. The number of apostleship.

*One of those days Jesus went out to a mountainside to pray, and spent
the night praying to God. When morning came, He called His disciples
to Him and chose twelve of them, whom He also designated apostles*
(Luke 6:12-13).

*Jesus said to them, "I tell you the truth, at the renewal of all things,
when the Son of Man sits on His glorious throne, you who have
followed Me will also sit on twelve thrones, judging the twelve tribes of
Israel"* (Matthew 19:28).

THIRTEEN: Thirteen evil thoughts from the heart listed. Rebellion or spiritual depravity.

For from within, out of men's hearts, come evil thoughts, sexual immorality, theft, murder, adultery, greed, malice, deceit, lewdness, envy, slander, arrogance and folly (Mark 7:21-22).

FOURTEEN: Deliverance or salvation. The number of double anointing.

Thus there were fourteen generations in all from Abraham to David, fourteen from David to the exile to Babylon, and fourteen from the exile to the Christ (Matthew 1:17).

FIFTEEN: Rest, mercy.

Mordecai recorded these events, and he sent letters to all the Jews throughout the provinces of King Xerxes, near and far, to have them celebrate annually the fourteenth and fifteenth days of the month of Adar as the time when the Jews got relief from their enemies, and as the month when their sorrow was turned into joy and their mourning into a day of celebration. He wrote them to observe the days as days of feasting and joy and giving presents of food to one another and gifts to the poor (Esther 9:20-22).

Say to the Israelites: "On the fifteenth day of the seventh month the Lord's Feast of Tabernacles begins, and it lasts for seven days. The first day is a sacred assembly; do no regular work" (Leviticus 23:34-35).

SIXTEEN: Love—sixteen things are said of love.

Love is patient, love is kind. It does not envy, it does not boast, it is not proud. It is not rude, it is not self-seeking, it is not easily angered, it keeps no record of wrongs. Love does not delight in evil but rejoices with the truth. It always protects, always trusts, always hopes, always perseveres. Love never fails. But where there are prophecies, they will cease; where there are tongues, they will be stilled; where there is knowledge, it will pass away (1 Corinthians 13:4-8).

SEVENTEEN: Immaturity. Transition. Victory.

Joseph, a young man of seventeen, was tending the flocks with his brothers, the sons of Bilhah and the sons of Zilpah, his father's wives, and he brought their father a bad report about them (Genesis 37:2).

Jacob lived in Egypt seventeen years, and the years of his life were a hundred and forty-seven (Genesis 47:28).

And on the seventeenth day of the seventh month the ark came to rest on the mountains of Ararat (Genesis 8:4).

EIGHTEEN: Bondage.

Then should not this woman, a daughter of Abraham, whom satan has kept bound for eighteen long years, be set free on the Sabbath day from what bound her? (Luke 13:16)

The Israelites were subject to Eglon king of Moab for eighteen years (Judges 3:14).

He became angry with them. He sold them into the hands of the Philistines and the Ammonites, who that year shattered and crushed them. For eighteen years they oppressed all the Israelites on the east side of the Jordan in Gilead, the land of the Amorites (Judges 10:7-8).

NINETEEN: Faith. Nineteen persons mentioned in Hebrews chapter 11.

Now faith is being sure of what we hope for and certain of what we do not see. This is what the ancients were commended for... (Hebrews 11:1-32).

TWENTY: Redemption (silver money in the Bible).

THIRTY: Blood of Jesus. Dedication. The beginning of service. Salvation.

Then one of the Twelve—the one called Judas Iscariot—went to the chief priests and asked, "What are you willing to give me if I hand Him over to you?" So they counted out for him thirty silver coins (Matthew 26:14-15).

Count all the men from thirty to fifty years of age who come to serve in the work in the Tent of Meeting. This is the work of the Kohathites in the Tent of Meeting: the care of the most holy things (Numbers 4:3-4).

Joseph was thirty years old when he entered the service of Pharaoh king of Egypt. And Joseph went out from Pharaoh's presence and traveled throughout Egypt (Genesis 41:46).

David was thirty years old when he became king, and he reigned forty years (2 Samuel 5:4).

FORTY: Trial. Probation. Testing or temptation.

Remember how the Lord your God led you all the way in the desert these forty years, to humble you and to test you in order to know what was in your heart, whether or not you would keep His commands. He humbled you, causing you to hunger and then feeding you with manna, which neither you nor your fathers had known, to teach you that man does not live on bread alone but on every word that comes from the mouth of the Lord. Your clothes did not wear out and your feet did not swell during these forty years. Know then in your heart that as a man disciplines his son, so the Lord your God disciplines you (Deuteronomy 8:2-5).

Jesus, full of the Holy Spirit, returned from the Jordan and was led by the Spirit in the desert, where for forty days He was tempted by the devil. He ate nothing during those days, and at the end of them He was hungry (Luke 4:1-2).

So he got up and ate and drank. Strengthened by that food, he traveled forty days and forty nights until he reached Horeb, the mountain of God (1 Kings 19:8).

On the first day, Jonah started into the city. He proclaimed: "Forty more days and Nineveh will be overturned" (Jonah 3:4).

FIFTY: Number of the Holy Spirit. Jubilee, liberty. The number for the Holy Spirit: He was poured out on the day of Pentecost which was fifty days after the resurrection of Christ.

Consecrate the fiftieth year and proclaim liberty throughout the land to all its inhabitants. It shall be a jubilee for you; each one of you is to return to his family property and each to his own clan (Leviticus 25:10).

SIXTY: Pride or arrogance. The image that Nebuchadnezzar set up was sixty cubits high.

Nebuchadnezzar the king made an image of gold, whose height was sixty cubits and its width six cubits. He set it up in the plain of Dura, in the province of Babylon (Daniel 3:1 NKJ).

SEVENTY: Universality or restoration. Israel lived in exile for seventy years after which they were restored.

In the first year of his reign, I, Daniel, understood from the Scriptures, according to the word of the Lord given to Jeremiah the prophet, that the desolation of Jerusalem would last seventy years (Daniel 9:2).

EIGHTY: Beginning of a high calling or becoming spiritually acceptable.

Moses was eighty years old when he started his ministry to deliver the Israelites.

NINETY OR NINETY-NINE: Fruits are ripe and ready. Abraham was ninety-nine years old when God appeared to him.

*When Abram was ninety-nine years old, the Lord appeared to him
and said, "I am God Almighty; walk before Me and be blameless"*
(Genesis 17:1 KJV).

ONE HUNDRED: God's election of grace. Children of promise. Full
reward. Abraham was one hundred years old when his son Isaac (child
of promise) was born.

Abraham was a hundred years old when his son Isaac was born to him
(Genesis 21:5).

ONE THOUSAND: The beginning of maturity; mature service or full
status.

Multiples or Complex Numbers

For these numbers, the meaning lies in the way it is pronounced rather
than as it is written.

Example:

2872 is pronounced "Two thousand, eight hundred, seventy-two."

Two thousand = confirmed spiritual maturity or mature judgment.

Eight hundred = new beginning into the promises.

Seventy-two = confirmed, completed, and restored.

Books by Dr. Joe Ibojie

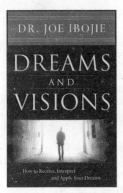

Dreams and Visions: How to receive, Interpret and Apply Your Dreams

Dreams and Visions presents sound scriptural principles and practical instructions to help us understand dreams and visions. It seeks to equip believers in the revelatory realm of dreams, their interpretation and usefulness in our everyday living. The book provides readers with the necessary understanding to approach dreams and visions by the Holy Spirit, through biblical illustrations, understanding of the meaning of dreams and prophetic symbolism, and by exploring the art of dream interpretation according to ancient methods of the Bible.

How to Live the Supernatural Life in the Here and Now

This book teaches you how to bring the Natural and the Supernatural to a place of balance in your life. Despite the tendency to live life in compartments, Dr. Ibojie believes that all of life is spiritual! The book will show you how to blend the Supernatural and the Natural, allowing you to function in harmony in all aspects of your life!

Order Now from Destiny Image Europe
Telephone: +39 085 4716623- Fax +39 085 4716622
E-mail: ordini@eurodestinyimage.com

Internet: www.eurodestinyimage.com

DREAM COURSES

Dreams are the parable language of God in a world that is spiritually distancing itself from experiencing the reality of His Presence. They are personalized, coded messages from God. Through dreams, God breaks through our thought processes, mindsets, prejudices and emotions to connect with the spirit of man. In this way He shows us what we might have missed or not heard or what our natural mind was incapable of comprehending. We all dream. He speaks to us at our individual levels and leads us further in Christ. God's ultimate purpose in dreams and visions is to align us to His plan and purposes in our lives!

The purpose of these courses is to equip the saints for the end-time move of God by learning the art of hearing Him and understanding how he speaks through dreams at an individual level.

Each dream course builds on the knowledge gained in the previous course. Attendees are strongly encouraged to take the courses in order for maximum effectiveness,

Topics to be covered include

COURSE 1

* Introduction to dreams and visions.
* Biblical history of dreams and visions.
* How dreams are received.
* Hindrances to receiving and remembering your dreams.
* How to respond to your dreams.
* Differences between dreams and visions.
* Introduction to interpreting your dreams.
* Understanding the ministry of angels.

COURSE 2

* Introduction to the language of symbols (the language of the spirit).
* Different levels of interpretation of dreams.
* Why we seek the meaning of our dreams.
* What to do with dreams you do not immediately understand.
* Maintaining and developing your dream-life.
* Expanding the scope of your dreams.
* Improving your interpretative skill.
* Visions and the Third Heaven.

COURSE 3

* Responding to revelations.
* Interpreting the dreams of others.
* Guidelines for setting up a corporate dream group.
* Prophetic symbolism.
* How to organize Dream Workshops.
* The Seer's anointing.
* The ministry of a Watchman.
* Spiritual warfare (fighting the good fight).
* Understanding the roles of angels and the different categories of angelic forces.
* How to work with angels.

COURSE 4

* Living the supernatural in the natural.
* Understanding the spiritual senses.
* Maintaining balance while blending the natural and the spiritual senses.
* Security and information management in revelatory ministry.
* Understanding the anointing.

* Dialoguing with God.
* An anatomy of Scriptural dreams.

WEEKEND COURSES

FRIDAY:
* Registration begins at 5:00 PM.
* Teaching begins at 6:00 PM.

SATURDAY:
* Registration begins at 9:00 AM.
* Sessions begin at 10:30 AM, 1:30 PM and 7:00 PM.

ONE WEEK COURSE (MONDAY TO FRIDAY)

Courses begin Monday morning and end Friday evening.

* Registration begins each day at 9:00 AM.
* Sessions begin at 10:00 AM and end at 5:00 PM.
There are breaks for lunch and tea.

The contents of each Dream Course will be covered in two weekend courses or a single one-week course (Monday to Friday).

To Request a DREAM COURSE in your area,
please call to arrange a program to fit your needs:

Dr Joe Ibojie
jcnibojie@hotmail.com
Phone: 44-77 6583 4253

Books to help you grow strong in Jesus

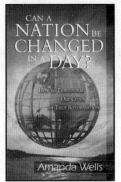

CAN A NATION BE CHANGED IN A DAY?

By Amanda Wells

A revolution is coming! The greatest reformation in earth's history is about to spread around the world. God's Kingdom is about to be established as never before imagined by God's people. God wants you to be a part of it! This exciting book reveals the hidden pattern of God's strategies of reformation through the words of the prophet Isaiah.

Using history and His Word as a foundation, this book proves how and why the world is about to experience a revolution of hope and transformation. It is a book that will encourage and ignite the Spirit of our loving heavenly Father within you.

ISBN:88-89127-11-2

CONFESSIONS OF A FASTING HOUSEWIFE

By Catherine Brown

This books is more than a spiritual guide to fasting— it is a practical primer on the "dos and don'ts" of fasting. Within these pages, Catherine Brown shares her experience in fasting in a 21st century world. Her humor, insight, and missteps during her sojourn will make you laugh—and empathize—with her plight as she discovers the emotional ups-and-downs of fasting. Spirituality and practically meet head-on in Confessions of a Fasting Housewife. Get ready to learn everything your pastor never told you about fasting! Then…fast!

ISBN:88-89127-10-4

Order Now from Destiny Image Europe
Telephone: +39 085 4716623- Fax +39 085 4716622
E-mail: ordini@eurodestinyimage.com
Internet: www.eurodestinyimage.com

Additional copies of this book and other book titles from DESTINY IMAGE EUROPE are available at your local bookstore.

We are adding new titles every month!

To view our complete catalog on-line, visit us at:
www.eurodestinyimage.com

Send a request for a catalog to:

Via Acquacorrente, 6
65123 - Pescara - ITALY
Tel. +39 085 4716623 - Fax +39 085 4716622

"Changing the world, one book at a time."

Are you an author?

Do you have a "today" God-given message?

CONTACT US

We will be happy to review your manuscript for a possible publishing:

publisher@eurodestinyimage.com